Acclaim for
Make Every Man Want You

"*Make Every Man Want You* is more than just a book about relationships. It's a book of empowerment for women of every age and lifestyle. As host of Web Sorority Talk Radio, I frequently hear successful women say that they wish they were as successful in love as they were in business. This book shows women the way to stop focusing on our little flaws and celebrate our strengths. Whether single or attached, this book is a must-read for every woman who wants to step into her power and start feeling great about herself!"

> —*Lynne Klippel,* author of **Web Wonder Women** and
> host of "Web Sorority Talk Radio"
> (websororitytalkradio.com)

"This book is brilliant! Simple, yet incredibly profound. If you are looking to be extremely desirable while building your confidence, devour every word in *Make Every Man Want You*—you'll be absolutely thrilled you did. Plus, you'll enjoy benefits for many years to come."

> —*Peggy McColl,* New York Times bestselling
> author of *Your Destiny Switch*

"Finally . . . a book that illustrates how developing an authentic relationship with your *self* is the core root of having great relationships with others. The concepts shared in *Make Every Man Want You* have helped me create a more positive, powerful self-awareness that immediately and noticeably changed the dynamics of my personal relationships."

—*Kendra Todd,* winner of "The Apprentice" (third season), bestselling author of *Risk & Grow Rich,* and host of HGTV's "My House Is Worth What?"

"Marie's *Make Every Man Want You* is an easy-to-read primer for any woman interested in feeling great and performing better in all areas of life. Don't think of this just as a dating book. Think of it as an engagement-to-a-better-lifestyle book."

—*David Greenwalt,* author of *The Leanness Lifestyle,* leannesslifestyle.com

"I am a psychotherapist who has spent years coaching people to overcome their blocks in relationships; Marie has hit the nail on the head and her book gives people the tools to connect with themselves, which is always the key to getting more out of life! Terrific book!"

—*Donna Fish,* L.C.S.W., author of *Take the Fight Out of Food,* takethefightoutoffood.com

"I am *blown away* by your book. It is *right on* and like a breath of *fresh air*—like you've given me permission to breathe. The freedom that this book will provide to all those that read it is astounding. This is a *must-read* for *all* women—whether there's a man in their life or not. *Thank you* for your amazing work and beautiful heart. I'm deeply moved and transformed from reading your book and ready to let the full irresistible me out there 24-7."

—*Lynn Rose,* motivational singer, speaker, and television and radio host, lynnrose.com

"What a fantastic, necessary tool for all us girls who need that little kick in the self-esteem pants! I'm Queen of the Worriers, so I love the fact that I *am* OK, and chilling out isn't optional to being irresistible, it's required."

—*Brett Jackson,* fashion and celebrity makeup artist

"My husband was shocked when he saw the book title, *Make Every Man Want You.* . . . He's singing a different tune now. The seemingly simple (but tremendously powerful) techniques in Marie's book actually brought an unexpected spark back to our marriage of seven and a half years. Trust me, what you'll learn will keep any man tickled pink . . . and you just may discover some new things about yourself. Excellent book!"

—*Lorrie Morgan-Ferrero,* copywriting expert and CEO of redhotcopy.com

"This is a great book for all women, in or out of relationships. I highly recommend reading and applying this material. I could not agree more with the information given and
look forward to practicing much of this in my own life!"

—*Heidi Selz,* cofounder of divaschool.com

"I'm a guy who dates lots of different women and I can say
that if a woman were to follow Marie's advice and be the
kind of woman Marie is describing, that woman would
be incredibly attractive. What Marie is talking about is a
woman being deeply and vibrantly *alive.* Everyone is drawn
to that—they can't help it. This is much more than a book
about dating strategies; it's a book about how to connect to
life's deepest treasures."

—*Will Morris,* CFM, financial adviser

"*Make Every Man Want You* will profoundly transform the way
you think and act in your relationships—and in your life.
Marie's highly effective strategies to experience true love,
authentic connection, and personal well-being are pure
magic! If you want the secret to truly winning in love and
life, read this book now."

—*Edward Hallowell,* M.D., bestselling author of
Crazy Busy and *Delivered from Distraction*

"*Make Every Man Want You* is a fantastic book! I loved every part of it. I feel strong and happy about myself and the world around me. I am reading it almost every day because it stays in my bag all the time. This book really changed my life. This is something every woman needs to know. Thanks for creating this amazing book!"

—*Silvana Jivkova,* entrepreneur, London, England

"I cannot thank you enough for writing a book like this. I must say this is one of the best investments I've ever made. Your work has truly opened my eyes to discover the life I have always wanted to live. I am now living a truly satisfying life, and those pointless issues from the past that I have no control over no longer even enter my mind-set. I look forward to any further material you make available. Once again, thank you!"

—*Andrew Mayne,* Victoria, Australia

"This book has quite simply changed my life! I have been able to go from struggling to get through each day to almost effortlessly creating what I want for my life. The changes are amazing, but what is most powerful is how quickly my life was transformed. *Make Every Man Want You* is so much more than a relationship book—it's an essential guide to living."

—*Virginia Daniels,* real estate developer and artist, Brisbane, Australia

Make
Every Man
Want You

Make
Every Man
Want You

How to Be So Irresistible You'll Barely Keep from Dating Yourself!

MARIE FORLEO

New York   Chicago   San Francisco   Lisbon   London   Madrid   Mexico City
Milan   New Delhi   San Juan   Seoul   Singapore   Sydney   Toronto

The *McGraw·Hill* Companies

Library of Congress Cataloging-in-Publication Data

Forleo, Marie.
  Make every man want you : how to be so irresistible you'll barely keep from dating
yourself! / Marie Forleo.
     p.   cm.
  Includes bibliographical references and index.
  ISBN 978-0-07-159781-4 (alk. paper)
     1. Dating (Social customs)   2. Man-woman relationships.   3. Women—
Psychology.   4. Self-confidence.   I. Title.

HQ801.F654   2008
646.7'7082—dc22   2007048921

19 20 LCR 21 20 19 18

ISBN 978-0-07-159781-4
MHID   0-07-159781-6

Interior design by Susan H. Hartman

McGraw-Hill books are available at special quantity discounts to use as premiums and
sales promotions or for use in corporate training programs. To contact a representative,
please visit the Contact Us pages at www.mhprofessional.com.

This book is printed on acid-free paper.

This book is dedicated to Josh.
I love you.

There cannot be too many glorious women.

—*Marianne Williamson,* author

Contents

Part 2 Eight Secrets to Magnetizing Men

Part 3 Pulling It All Together

Acknowledgments

hank you, dear reader, for investing in this powerful and enlivening guide to unleashing your irresistibility. This book was written with your greatness in
mind.

Thanks to my many teachers and mentors who have
shared their wisdom through classes, books, audio programs, phone calls, and meals. I am grateful for the wisdom you have passed on and kept alive throughout the
ages.

Finally, many thanks to my invaluable and loving
community of family, friends, clients, and colleagues, for
listening, supporting, encouraging, and cheering me on.
Especially Josh Pais, Ron Forleo, Miriam Forleo, Ronny
Forleo, Kelli Dalrymple, Marc Santa Maria, Donna Cyrus,
Fernanda Franco, Lenore Pemberton, Caitlin Ward, Rod-
erick Hill, TAG Online, Lynne Klippel, Deborah-Miriam
Leff, Bill Gladstone, Waterside Productions, John Aherne,

McGraw-Hill, the girls (Melissa, Ginger, Simone, Tracy, Semira, Michelle, and Kristin), Monika Batista, the Tuesday Night DTW Dancers, the Crunch Dancers, Crunch Fitness, Joe Polish, Piranha Marketing, the entire Transformational Community, and, last but certainly not least, Ariel and Shya Kane—I love you guys!

Preface

$\mathcal{W}$hat if I told you that, in about an hour, I could share information with you that could make you happier, healthier, and more attractive in a matter of minutes?

What if I told you this same information could transform the quality of your love life forever?

What if you knew the secret to being irresistibly attractive and what it takes to enjoy healthy, satisfying relationships without being manipulative or fake?

What if you didn't have to play games, follow rules, or be calculating to get what you want?

Would you be interested? Would you spend an hour or so with me? Would you like to be so damn irresistible you'll barely keep from dating yourself?

If the idea of being authentic, expressive, and irresistible is of interest to you—and I hope it is—then you are in the right place. *Make Every Man Want You* is designed to incite a complete life transformation. You'll find new possibilities you've never before imagined at work, at play, with family and friends—and all without requiring very much effort on your part (don't you just love that?).

You may wonder about the title, *Make Every Man Want You*. You may say, "I don't want every man to want me—just one good man would be enough!" Well, I have a confession. I've whipped up an intriguing title to trick you into reading this book. You see, what you're about to learn is a radical new approach to being completely irresistible, inside and out, and how to have magnificent relationships with everyone in your life.

Some of what you are about to learn will be the complete opposite of what you have believed or been taught in the past about relationships. You have got to keep in mind that you would not be reading this book unless there was some aspect of your ability to relate that wasn't working for you.

Here is my first tip: when something does not work in your life, assume that you are operating on false information. Don't worry—this is not a problem. In fact, it is a blessing. It means you have become aware that you are off track and have already taken the first step to correct course.

With an open mind and willingness to lead an irresistible lifestyle, you're about to discover a whole new I-can't-believe-it-could-be-this-good world of love, relationship, and authentic partnership that is available and waiting for you.

How to Get the Most Out of This Book

This book is designed to enlighten, entertain, and transform. Where appropriate, I've included thought-provoking questions to spark insight and irresistible action challenges to help you implement this material in order to create lasting and meaningful shifts in your life.

If you'd like some extra guidance and support, I've created a free online Irresistible Action Guide that includes all the exercises in this book as well as a complimentary four-week audio coaching program to help you stay inspired and on track. Go to makeeverymanwantyou.com/actionguide to download these bonus resources and find more info.

Remember, reading and understanding something is light-years away from actually doing it. I could read how-to-write-a-self-help-book books all day long and understand that I need to have an idea, an outline, a computer, and a printer. But if I don't sit myself down and actually write, that self-help book will never come into existence! Same thing applies to you, dear reader. You must practice being irresistible if you really want to make every man want you. Intellectualizing is not enough.

This book is about using awareness to melt away previously hidden tendencies and behaviors that sabotage your relationships. In my experience, when you become aware of a behavior that's been getting in your way and simply notice it—without judging yourself for what you discover—that behavior melts away on its own. Nonjudgmental awareness facilitates effortless resolution. Seeing is really enough. When you see yourself, without judgment, you dissolve the conditioning from your past.

This approach is not about setting a goal to be who you think would be a better, more irresistible you. When you set out to be better or get better, two things happen. First, you're making a blanket statement into the universe that you are broken and need fixing. This keeps you locked in a dissatisfying mental thought loop of "I'm not good enough yet." Second, you'll likely resist those habits or tendencies that your mind considers bad, and because (as you'll learn) anything we resist persists, those habits and tendencies tend to stick around. Want proof? Just take a look at how often you've made and stuck to New Year's resolutions and you'll see that the be-a-better-you approach is not extremely effective.

You may be thinking, "I'm confused. How can I notice something I'm doing to get in my own way without judging it or making a statement into the universe that something's wrong with me?" Here's how.

Adopt a gentle, inquisitive approach to self-discovery. Be innocently curious. When you see something about yourself, say, "Oh . . . interesting" or "Huh, look at that." Simply observe what exists without trying to change it. Stop pressuring yourself to embody some elusive, idealized standard you've created in your mind of the "perfect" you. Despite popular belief, you can be fully invested in growth and learning without having an underlying problem to fix.

For example, I know I'm a good dancer and I'm always willing to expand my abilities. When I find a new dance move challenging, I investigate to see if there's something I may be doing (or not doing) that's preventing me from getting the move. I try different things with my body. I may ask other dancers and teachers for help. I'm truly interested in seeing, growing, and learning. Sometimes I find the move through my own exploration; other times a fellow dancer is able to point out what I can't see on my own. Then I say, "Oh. I see now. Thanks." And that's enough. Transformation. Expansion. Growth. And all done from a spirit of self-discovery—not self-reproach.

The fastest way to see results in this or any other program is to team up with other people. Countless studies prove that those who exercise with partners tend to lose weight faster, keep it off longer, and feel more satisfied and supported in the process. Being irresistibly "in shape" is no different. When you connect with others, you drop unwanted behaviors faster, stay true to yourself more consistently, and feel a greater sense of love and support along the way.

Talk about what you learn with friends, sisters, brothers, coworkers, moms, coaches—anyone with whom you feel a special connection. The magic that is produced when two or more people come together to hold a shared vision is miraculous.

This book is yours. Use it fully. Try on the concepts. Complete every exercise. Experiment and discover your truth. Allow the magic on these pages to support you in expressing the power, enchantment, and sensuality you have waiting inside.

The world needs that smart, funny, beautiful woman you've been dying to unleash. It's my honor to show you the way. Let's go!

The Make Every Man Want You Story

Make Every Man Want You began as a little e-book project more than six years ago. I was in my early twenties, engaged, and living with my fiancé in a tiny one-room West Village apartment in New York City. I had just started life coaching after leaving jobs on Wall Street, in fashion, and in advertising. I was eager to write a book and start making my mark on the world. What better topic than—you guessed it—women and relationships! There was only one small problem: my own relationship.

Here I was—a young, successful, attractive woman with a big diamond ring, joint bank accounts, a handsome and sweet fiancé, an entire group of friends and family excitedly looking forward to a wedding—and all I could think about was how to get the hell out of it. How could I possibly promote a book about relationships when mine was in shambles? I simply couldn't do it. The *Make Every Man Want You* e-book got pulled from the Internet and filed away on a hard drive.

Deep down, I knew I needed to get out of this engagement, but for six long months I was too scared to do it. What would I say? Where would I live? What would happen to my career? What would my parents think of me? What would everyone else think of me? What would I think of me?

With each passing day, the lie I was living grew bigger, more painful, and more overwhelming. The fights I had with my fiancé swelled to the point that it was almost unbearable to share the same space. Then one morning everything shifted. I woke up and thought, "This cannot go on for one more second. I need to end this right here and right now. My life depends on it." I can't remember exactly what I said, but I know that as soon as the words "It's over" came out of my mouth, I felt a surge of relief and exhilaration like nothing I'd ever experienced before. Of course, we cried as I handed back the ring, but deep inside I knew that this was the best decision for both of us.

Ever since that moment, things have never been the same. It's as though my soul recalibrated once I found the courage to speak my truth. I began investing in personal growth seminars and did everything I could to discover what it takes to live a truly magnificent life. I was especially interested in how to have relationships that really work and in what it takes to be fulfilled and satisfied on a consistent basis. I read tons of books, went to countless seminars, and hired the best coaches I could find. What happened next was absolutely miraculous.

My life, which was never bad to begin with, completely transformed into something utterly magical. Out of a willingness to really investigate how I was operating in my life and see my part in things, all the personal and professional success that had eluded me for so long finally clicked into place.

First of all, I met an incredible man named Josh, with whom I formed a committed relationship. He's like a dream come true (truth be told, he's even better). He's creative, supportive, honest, successful, loving, and funny beyond belief. Second, a seemingly impossible dream I had held for so long came into reality (and very quickly, I might add). Ever since I was a little girl, I wanted to be a dancer. Never having had any formal training, I thought that at age twenty-six I was too old to begin. Well, within months of taking my first class, I began teaching and shortly after was hired by MTV as a choreographer, producer, and performer. Before long I was teaching and presenting internationally and since then have led thousands of women and men around the world through classes, workshops, and special events. I work regularly with amazing magazines like *Self*, *Women's Health*, and *Prevention* and organizations like Crunch Fitness and Nike. At the time of this writing, I have created and led four top-selling dance and fitness DVDs and am proud to be a Nike Elite Athlete and Master Trainer.

About a year ago, I thought, "Wow, this investigating your life stuff really does work!" For the first time ever, I felt an authentic sense of clarity and awareness. Excited to share what I had discovered and experienced, I reenergized my life-coaching practice. My clients began having success and satisfaction like never before, and I knew it was time to write the new and improved version of *Make Every Man Want You.*

Everything that I discovered, everything that shifted my life so dramatically—especially my ability to have relationships that actually work—you are about to learn for yourself in this book. But hold on, because this gets even better.

The very same principles that transform your love life will spill over into every other area of your life as well. Your career, finances, health, and sense of well-being, as well as your relationships with family, friends, and colleagues, will all be stronger and more satisfying than you could ever imagine. I've done my best to leave nothing out because I want to make your irresistible transformation as easy and effortless as possible. So are you ready? It's time for your first lesson: Irresistibility 101.

Make
Every Man
Want You

Part 1

Keys to Making Every Man (and Everyone Else) Want You

||||||||||||||||||||||||||||||||||||||||||||

If you have knowledge, let others light their candles in it.

—Margaret Fuller, author and philosopher

Chapter 1

Irresistibility 101

> Take the first step in faith. You don't have to see
> the whole staircase. Just take the first step.
>
> —*Dr. Martin Luther King Jr.*

Have you ever had the feeling that you were meant for great things? As a little girl, did you know you had something special to express into the world? Many of us have lost touch with our whimsical, feminine dreams of greatness in exchange for a more driven, masculine take on success. Without even knowing it, we've been enlisted on a mission: to prove we can do it as well as, or better than, the men. We are all so desperate to attain what we imagine will make us equal and happy (a successful career, marriage, family, 2.2 kids) that we forget who we really are: brilliant, sexy, and magical beings like no other.

We've forgotten that our power lies not in competing with or trying to be like men but in embracing our natural and womanly strengths of compassion, enchantment, and tenderness. We are intuitive healers and masterful lovers. Our hearts run deep with emotion, and we cast a wide net for spiritual truth. Our sexuality and feminine wiles inspire, enliven, and empower. We are remarkable.

The world is in desperate need of irresistible women: women who are willing to be enthusiastic, alive, and expressive—regardless of the circumstance; women who are not afraid to tell their truth or speak up for what they believe in; women who feel at ease being intelligent, sensual, and compassionate all at once; women who do not compete with, demean, or do battle against men (or other women) but who see everyone for who they really are—fellow human beings also in search of a great life, in search of love.

Let's face it: love is all we really want. Although we strive for the right clothes, the right hair, the right body, the right job, the right relationship, what we really want is to know someone loves us and everything's going to be OK.

You know what? You are loved and you are OK right now. Everything else is an illusion. Worry, regret, and anxiety are all mental constructions called up by our minds to distract us from the terrifying realization that underneath it all, we're just fine. As we relax and embrace our own OK-ness, we unlock our irresistibility. Our dreams surge back into our hearts, and our spirits are free to soar once again. Without so much energy tied up in our imagined neuroses, we have the time and energy to reengage with our purpose and once again make a difference in our world. You are an extraordinary woman. You have a purpose in this world, and hiding behind a fictional story that you're broken or incomplete is not it. The world needs you. It needs that very special something you knew you had when you were a little girl.

Claiming your irresistibility is the key to fulfilling your potential as a woman and as a human being. It's the secret to making the impact on the world you were meant to make. Women who embrace their irresistibility hold the heart of the world.

Fully embrace your feminine as well as your masculine energies. We all have both, and integrating them in a balanced way is the key to unlocking your full potential as a human being. Follow as much as you lead. Comfort as much as you command. Dance with the ever-changing flow of both masculine and feminine energies within you, and allow the fullness of your glory as an irresistible woman to show through in everything you do. Your feminine side is more compelling than you could ever imagine. Your softness and vulnerability are magnificent. You are an irresistible woman. Be proud. Whether it's in the boardroom or the bedroom, on the battlefield or in the grocery store, our world needs irresistible women now more than ever. Our children need them. Our businesses need them. Our schools need them. Our governments need them. The world needs you to claim your brilliance and share it. Let your life be an example of how glorious it is to be an irresistible woman.

Irresistibility 101 lays groundwork for having a brilliant life and magical relationships and, of course, for being authentically irresistible. The purpose of this chapter is to open your mind to new possibilities and greater personal awareness. Awareness is the key that allows you to stop automatically doing things that drive men away and begin naturally doing things that support happy and satisfying relationships. Master this stuff and you'll notice that men, women, children, small animals, large animals, dust bunnies, and anything else that's not glued down will find it virtually impossible to resist you.

Your Irresistibility Lies in the Present Moment

Take a deep breath and let your shoulders melt down. Relax your jaw and ease into the moment. Allow yourself simply to be here. Forget about your to-do lists. Let go of wandering thoughts of what you might have for dinner or regrets about what you didn't get done today at work.

Your ability to be completely irresistible and make every man want you lies in the present moment. When you are fully present (meaning your full attention is in "the now"), you access the infinite source of beauty and aliveness inherent in every living creature. You become one with the cosmic intelligence and timeless magnificence of all that is.

On a physiological level, being present means that you stop going on mental vacations and actively engage your mind, body, and soul in whatever you are doing in this moment. You let go of thoughts about the past and worries about the future and bring your full attention to whatever, or whoever, is in front of you right now. In the context of reading this book, being present means giving your full, undivided attention to "hearing" the words on the page as you read them.

Refrain from the temptation to compare this to other self-help books you've read or to wonder whether or not this will work for you. All that mental chatter pulls you out of the moment and away from your irresistibility. Listening to that conversation you have with yourself is what has gotten you lost and confused in the first place.

Here's a nugget of wisdom that can transform your life in an instant. Ready?

You are not your mind.

You have a mind, but you are not your mind. You are also not the conversation you have with yourself in your mind. You may be thinking, "What conversation? What is she talking about?" *That* one!

Of course, you may be thinking, "Well then, who *am* I?" Who you are is a glorious being behind your mind. You are the awareness, the observer, the listener. You are the wise, elegant, generous, and loving consciousness that knows exactly what I'm talking about right now.

Know this, too: your irresistibility is greatest when you're present and disengaged from your mental chatter. That's because the fullness and glory of your being is showing through. Your being is your highest self and grandest expression of who you are. It is timeless and beautiful, full of love, compassion, forgiveness, and sensuality. It needs nothing and seeks no approval. It is who you really are beneath all of the worry, concern, and fear.

Your mind, on the other hand, is a past/future fear-based machine that is primarily concerned with survival. It's always comparing, analyzing, scheming, and talking to you about what you need to do in order to become better, prettier, more successful, or more attractive. The mind is usually not supportive of your irresistibility. It likes to talk about your mistakes and how bad, unattractive, stupid, or unworthy you are. (By the way, none of those things your mind talks to you about are actually true, but unless you become aware that you are not your mind, you believe them to be true.)

The real truth is that it doesn't matter how many mistakes you've made in the past or how many relationships have not worked out. It also doesn't matter how much you weigh, how old you are, or what you do for a living. You can be absolutely irresistible starting right now. The rest of this book will show you how.

Everything Is as It Should Be

There are no coincidences. What you have in your life you attracted to yourself, consciously or unconsciously. Everything is exactly as it should be. Every joy, challenge, opportunity, and circumstance—including the fact that you are reading this book—is exactly what you need to serve your own personal, irresistible evolution. None of this is coincidence.

Many women struggle against what's happening in their lives, as though things should be different. They don't recognize that when one struggles against the moment, one actually struggles against the entire universe. This constant battle of resistance is deadly to our irresistibility. Every bit of disappointment, anger, pain, upset, and disharmony we experience is a result of our resistance to, or disagreement with, some current aspect of our life.

Conversely, when we stop resisting or disagreeing with how our life is showing up and truly surrender to the fact that everything is as it should be, we get back in sync with the universe and have instant access to greater personal power, clarity, and irresistibility.

It's important to note that understanding "everything is as it should be" does not mean you roll over and play dead, stay in an abusive or unloving relationship, or become complacent. Acknowledging reality empowers you. It puts you in the driver's seat of your life and turns the ignition.

The practice of acknowledging reality is called making is-ness your business. In other words, get more interested in reality, or what is, rather than complaining or wishing things would be different. (Side note: the notion of is-ness has been mentioned in everything from religion to spirituality to self-improvement to science. While I didn't create it, I do find it incredibly useful, as will you.)

In short, here's what making is-ness your business means: engage in your life with enthusiasm exactly as it is, regardless of your likes and dislikes, your preferences, ideas, beliefs, and opinions about how things should be or could be. Unconditionally allow things to be the way they are. When you deal with what is, or your is-ness, you can then choose who you'd like to be in relationship to that.

Making is-ness your business is the secret to being powerful and magnetic in your life. When you consistently engage with your life exactly as it is—not as you would prefer it—you're no longer held hostage by your circumstances or victimized by the world. Here's an example. Let's say you're stuck in traffic. Being in gridlock, at that moment, is your is-ness. Of course, you don't prefer to be stuck in traffic, but that is how it is. You have two choices: you can moan and complain about it (resist your is-ness) or you can surrender (make is-ness your business) and enjoy it. Enjoying it may look like listening to the radio and rocking it out to your favorite tunes (what I affectionately call car dancing), listening to educational or personal development CDs, making phone calls that need to be handled, or simply relaxing back into your seat. What I find so powerful is that very often, when I genuinely surrender to traffic, not only does my frustration quickly subside, but the traffic also begins moving quite quickly again as well.

Important caveat: you can't practice making is-ness your business as a manipulation to make a situation

improve or get better. You've got to genuinely give it a
go. Only then will the magic happen. Understanding this
universal truth is essential to the Make Every Man Want
You approach because this is your access point to full
personal blossoming.

############### **Irresistible Insight Questions** ###############

1. Have you noticed that when you resist your is-ness,
   the result is always frustration? Can you see that
   arguing with what is only produces pain and misery,
   especially in you?

2. How would your life shift if you made is-ness your
   business all the time? Do you think you'd be more
   or less loving? More or less effective? More or less
   irresistible?

3. What is your relationship like right now? Not what
   it should be if the two of you could stop arguing or
   could be if he had more money but what it actually is
   at this moment. Can you stop holding back and start
   loving? What kind of impact would compassion have
   on your relationship?

4. Are you willing to give up frustration and anger in
   lieu of a new possibility? How good will you allow
   your life to be?

Where Our Ideas Come From

As a kid, I loved music. One song that brings back fond memories was by an artist named Falco. He had a very catchy tune that I used to sing and dance to. At nine years old, I especially liked the fact that he had a thick foreign

Irresistible Action Challenge

For the next twenty-four hours, make is-ness your total business. No matter what happens—your printer breaks, your date cancels, or the plane is delayed for two hours— pretend that you wanted it to happen. You can even say, "And this is what I want!" after any circumstance that your mind wants to resist. For example:

You're on hold for forty-five minutes with your cell phone provider. Say to yourself, "Huh . . . I've been on hold for forty-five minutes . . . and this is what I want!" Then, when you lose your signal and get disconnected just as you're about to speak with a customer service rep, say, "Huh . . . just got disconnected . . . and this is what I want." While it may feel slightly kooky, this exercise not only will give you a laugh but will also help you become aware of all the ways you resist your is-ness and unwittingly create misery, frustration, and upset in your life.

accent and sang about hot potatoes (an odd choice I thought, but hey—it was the '80s, and he was Austrian). It went something like this:

"Hot potatoes, hot potatoes, hot po-ta-toes, hot potatoes, hot potatoes—oh oh oh, hot potatoes . . ." The song had a really funky electronic sound, and in the summer of 1985, when I was nine years old, I thought it was cool. Fast-forward nine years. I was watching a "Top Hits of the '80s" music video special on MTV when they announced Falco was up next. "Cool," I thought. "I'll finally get to see why this guy sings about hot potatoes."

Well, to my surprise and embarrassment, the song had nothing at all to do with hot potatoes. The song was called "Rock Me Amadeus." At nine years old, I had never heard of Amadeus—it wasn't in my vocabulary yet. My young mind filled in with something that sounded familiar (hot potatoes), and until I learned otherwise, I believed Falco's hit was about steaming spuds.

The point of this story is to illustrate that everything we know is simply a collection of thoughts and information we have absorbed over our lifetime. Most of us never investigate whether those thoughts and that information are actually accurate. When it comes to men and relationships, most of us have absorbed ideas that not only are inaccurate but also undermine our ability to enjoy a healthy and satisfying love life.

Let's face it: your parents probably didn't take a How to Have Wonderful Relationships course in school. How about your grandparents? Did they have Loving and Lasting Relationships 101? Doubt it. They learned from their parents, who learned from their parents, and so on and so forth, all the way back in time.

While it's not your fault, or anyone else's, that you've been operating on some erroneous information about relationships that's been passed down since the beginning of time, it's now your responsibility to step up and use what works. As Maya Angelou says, "Now you know better, so you do better."

Investigate Your Thinking Problem

The first step in kicking a drinking problem is to admit you have one. Well, most women, myself included, have some form of a "thinking" problem—especially when it comes to men and relationships. We think excessively, and much of our thinking is repetitive, illusory, and downright toxic. So the first step in kicking our thinking problem is to admit that we have one.

It has been said that humans have approximately fifty to sixty thousand thoughts per day and 95 percent of those thoughts are the same ones we had yesterday. This means that unconsciously, we're all feeding ourselves the same inaccurate information over and over again. No wonder nothing ever seems to change.

The way out is through awareness. Be willing to investigate how your mind and belief system are currently configured around men and relationships. Take a look at what you believe and why you believe it in the first place. Ask yourself, "Who put that thought there? Who said so? Is it serving me?" Regarding the last question, my guess is that, for the most part, it's not.

Now let's investigate what you know about relationships. As we discovered earlier with my "hot potatoes" lyrics, much of what we believe to be true is simply an old collection of thoughts put together by a younger, less experienced version of ourselves.

When it comes to men and relationships, our ideas are often put in place during an upsetting situation, such as a breakup. Ideas like:

- I can't trust men.
- I'm not pretty/skinny/talented/funny enough.
- All men cheat.
- Relationships are hard work.
- I'll never find someone.

It's during times of disappointment that we make decisions in our minds that limit what is possible for us in the future. The problem is that we often forget those decisions were made, yet as we move forward in time, those old decisions hold us back from feeling fully alive and capable of truly connecting in our relationships.

Much like an old computer, our minds have outdated software. Investigating our thinking problem is akin to getting a much-needed software upgrade. As we look, we'll see that the information our minds contain—especially about men and relationships—is not only outdated but also completely contradictory to what we say we want now. See for yourself. Quickly complete the following sentences:

Love is _____.

Good men are _____.

I'll bet you had some automatic responses, like "blind" and "hard to find." Even if we don't believe those statements to be true, our minds, like the autofill function on computers, automatically fill in the blanks based on information we've put there or heard before. If you want to make every man want you, you've got to bring awareness to your thinking problem and get clean. Remaining unaware that you are holding on to old ideas only keeps you stuck in the past and out of the present, where more fulfilling and expansive relationship possibilities exist.

Being Irresistible Requires Personal Responsibility

Personal responsibility means being accountable for the results that do or do not show up in your life. More specifically, responsibility means you have the ability to respond

Irresistible Action Challenge

What are some ideas about love, men, and relationships you hold as "the truth"? What types of things were you told by family and friends? What old decisions about men or relationships have you made during an upsetting experience? Take a few minutes and write down what you believe to be "the truth."

Now look at your first "truth" and answer the following questions. Then go back and review the questions for each old "truth" you wrote down. How old were you when you first had that idea? Is it serving you now? How willing are you to kick your thinking problem and reclaim your irresistibility?

to your life instead of automatically react to it. Many of us behave like robots, mechanically acting out habitual thought patterns of self-pity, overwhelming resentment, and wishful thinking. Rather than discovering who we are now or who we are with now, we re-act, or act again, based on how we reacted to similar events in our past.

Women often unleash old anger and resentment from the past on people they are currently dating. This commonly includes grievances held against former boyfriends, husbands, and bosses and, particularly, gripes with Dad.

This automatic behavior kills our irresistibility. It is also why many women keep having the same relationships over and over again with different men. They keep re-acting out of old, robotic habits and repeatedly produce similar, undesirable results with every man they meet. Rather than taking responsibility and investigating how they operate to see what they are doing (or not doing), they find it easier to place the blame on the "bad man" or on "bad luck."

Being personally responsible allows you to dissolve old programming and start responding to your life appropriately rather than mechanically re-acting like you did in the past. This is an incredibly exciting place to live. With personal responsibility, you gain a tremendous amount of control in your life. You can free yourself from cyclical life patterns and proactively impact the quality and existence of your relationships.

The first step in personal responsibility is to bring awareness to how you operate in your life. This means being investigative, observant, and nonjudgmental. My good friends Ariel and Shya Kane, internationally acclaimed authors and seminar leaders, teach an easy and effective way to do this: pretend you're an anthropologist studying a culture of one—you.

The Kanes encourage an anthropological approach to life. Anthropologists simply note what is. They look and observe without adding commentary or judgment. For example, an anthropologist would never say, "Those crazy

savages perform ridiculous fire dances at ungodly hours."
An anthropologist would simply jot down, "The indigenous
people perform fire rituals at 3:00 A.M."

If you want to be irresistibly attractive, you have to
observe yourself in this same nonjudgmental way. Simply notice what you do. When you judge, berate, criticize,
complain, or otherwise add commentary to your self-
observations, you actually cement undesirable behaviors in
place.

The challenge, of course, is that our minds are automatic
judgment machines. They instantly evaluate everything we
do as either good or bad, right or wrong. Thankfully, this
isn't a problem. The trick is to simply notice the judgment
and then not judge yourself for judging yourself. And if
that doesn't work (you continue to judge yourself for judging yourself) take one step out and don't judge yourself for
judging yourself for judging yourself. At some point, you'll
reach a state of neutrality.

There's a law in physics that states that for every action,
there is an equal and opposite reaction. In other words,
what we resist persists. Judging, berating, criticizing, and
complaining are all forms of resisting. They are nonneu-
tral statements that act like Krazy Glue and stick your
unwanted behavioral patterns to you. When you simply
notice what you do instead of judge or criticize yourself, a
magical transformation takes place instantly. You will no
longer be run by the habitual behaviors that kill your irre-

sistibility and cause relationship mischief. This is because what you nonjudgmentally look at disappears.

Looking at something without judging it is neutral and liberating. If you nonjudgmentally observe a behavior, you will have introduced choice into the equation. In that moment, you are free (if you so choose) to stop doing those things that kill your attractiveness. Being nonjudgmental instantly dissolves the habitual nature of your behaviors and creates the option for you to be authentically, appropriately, and irresistibly you.

If there's any situation or circumstance in your life that you don't like (for example, being single, out of shape, shy around men, in a mediocre relationship), you're resisting it. Said another way, when you resist something, you actually add energy to it by thinking about how much you don't like it or wish it would be over already. This keeps re-creating it in your experience, and pretty soon, it's all you can think about.

When you simply look at a situation, see it as it is, and stop wishing it were different, the situation loses its dominating power over you. The problematic aspect of it disappears. You lighten up and interact more lovingly with your life and the people in it. By being aware of what is without resisting it, your unconditioned consciousness is awakened. You can see more clearly and compassionately. Your ability to be effective instantly expands. It is from this place of neutral awareness that your true irresistibility is unleashed and the following can occur:

- Being single is no longer a problem or failing you have to get over. It's an opportunity to reengage in your life and reinvest in your spiritual growth. It's a jump-off point for fun, adventure, romance, and self-discovery.

- Being out of shape is no longer a permanent character flaw. It's simply your current starting place from which to reveal a stronger, healthier, and more fit you.

- Being in an unsatisfying relationship is not something you have to make different (that is, you needn't try to change your man into something he's not). Tell the truth that it doesn't work for you anymore, and give yourself the option to create something that does work.

Contrary to popular belief, you do not need years of therapy to heal yourself or change undesired behaviors. With awareness (again, which is a judgment-free noticing of something), resolution can occur instantly.

Reality check: does this mean that if you are $26,000 in debt and you look at it nonjudgmentally, it will literally disappear? I wish. What will happen, however, is that you will no longer be dominated by the guilt, worry, and fear associated with it. You'll get your life back and regain your personal power. By noticing the is-ness of your debt, you can begin taking action to reduce it. The universe will support you with a bigger tax refund, a raise, new clients, or other "found" money. In the meantime, you will no longer live under the constant mental chatter about how "bad" you are for having debt or live your life through a filter of scarcity.

The first step is personal responsibility. And the key to personal responsibility is awareness. When you become aware of things you do that are not conducive to attracting and keeping men, and don't judge yourself for what you discover, you actually stop doing those things.

The Irresistible Paradox: You're Already Irresistible and There's More to Come

A paradox is a statement that initially appears to be contradictory but then, upon closer inspection, turns out to be true. Most women I know are truly irresistible, but they just don't know it yet. They walk around with false and outdated ideas of who they are and look for validation in places it can never be found—such as the right body, a successful career, or the perfect relationship.

The truth is your irresistibility is independent of the physical world and your life circumstances. It is ageless and outside the confines of time and space. You are not separate from it. You do not have to be someone else or do anything additional to access it. You simply need to remember your true nature, your being, and be willing to look at the obstacles that have gotten in your way without judging yourself for what you discover.

You've already taken the first step. You've had the courage and desire to invest in this book. That tells me you are willing to investigate your own personal landscape and take the exciting journey of self-realization.

I tell you this: your irresistibility is already within; however, there is certain information you're currently unaware of that's sabotaging its full bloom. And, although you're already irresistible, there's always more that's possible. Your potential is limitless, and you will continue to discover deeper facets of your aliveness if you are willing to keep investing in yourself and practice the irresistible lifestyle outlined in this book. Make no mistake. There is *no limit* to how radiant, alive, and irresistible you can be.

Satisfying and Loving Relationships Are Your Birthright

You deserve healthy, satisfying, and loving relationships. They are your birthright. God (a.k.a. the goddess, the universe, higher power, the source, or whatever you like to call him or her) created you—and everything else in our universe—in complete perfection. By virtue of having been born, you are loved. It is not something you have to earn, manipulate, or figure out how to produce. It's hardwired into you. You are not separate from love.

In a certain respect, love is all there is. Fear, resentment, isolation, and aloneness are all illusions created by the mind to keep us believing we are separate from one another and separate from our divinity. The mind needs this belief to survive. The mind thrives on it. Your being, however, knows that underneath the illusion of the mind, love is all there is. Your being knows there is no limit on love's supply. Love will never run out and it can never be stolen from you, because you are the source. Giving it away only produces more. Remember this as you meet the obstacles to your irresistibility. Love is the fuel that energizes the world and can transform all darkness into light. Let it fuel you past the false thoughts and old ideas that have shadowed your true irresistible nature up until now.

Irresistibility Is a Lifestyle, Not a One-Time Magic Pill

You're discovering how to naturally unleash your irresistibility, inside and out. It is the greatest gift you can give yourself and the world. But being irresistible is a lifestyle, not a one-time magic pill. It's like being in great physical shape. You can't exercise once and then never go to the gym again and expect to be fit. Lasting results of health, fitness, and well-being come from consistency over time. Being irresistibly "fit" is no different.

A lifestyle, by definition, is a way of life or style of living that reflects the attitudes and values of a person. The irre-

sistible lifestyle is about being fully alive, expressive, and
compassionate (to yourself and others). It's about accessing
your highest self and living consistently with awareness.

The irresistible lifestyle can be easily forgotten when
life throws you a curveball. You lose your job. Your printer
goes on strike right before a big meeting. The new guy who
seemed so dreamy turns out to be a royal jerk. When you
get upset or disappointed, it's normal to get knocked off
center and forget your true irresistible nature. It's tempting
to slip back into old, unattractive, familiar habits. I'm not
suggesting that you pretend everything's rosy when it's not.
What I am suggesting is that you don't hang out there.

Build your irresistible lifestyle muscles by following
these three steps:

1. Practice neutrally observing what you feel.
   Acknowledge your emotions. Tell the truth.
   Report your inner reality without adding a layer
   of drama or victimhood over it.

2. Allow yourself to really feel it without trying to
   make the feeling different than it is or attempting
   to get over it. Experience the physical sensation.
   Watch what's happening on an emotional level
   without getting lost in the mechanical thoughts
   triggered by your mind.

3. Keep bringing yourself back to this moment and
   respond (not react) from there.

Please don't misunderstand. I'm not suggesting that you pretend to be happy when you're not or that you don't speak your mind when something's not working for you. What I am proposing is another possibility: a space of irresistibility where you can be authentic, communicate your truth fully, and enjoy a sense of well-being all at the same time.

Don't forget your true nature. It's during challenging times that we most need to remember how brilliant we really are. Support yourself back to center by rereading this book and others that leave you feeling inspired and alive. Reach out. Call your coach or others who can help you get back on track. Use this work to create a community of irresistible women (and men) who will support each other in living from their brilliance, not their victimhood.

Just like working out, these practices will build your irresistibility muscles. You'll develop strength and stamina over time. When you get bumped off course, you'll be able to quickly and easily regain your center. Your intrinsic nature is irresistibility. It is healing, both for you and for the world. Make it a lifestyle.

$\mathcal{N}$o Manipulations, Tricks, or Techniques

Being authentically irresistible is not about how to manipulate men or do little tricks or techniques to get them to love you. After all, if you have to manipulate, perform trickery, or master techniques to get someone to love you, he doesn't love the real you.

He's fallen for a well-executed technique. And what's worse, if you use manipulation or tricks to catch a man, you'll have to keep up a 24-7 charade so he'll never catch a glimpse of the real you. (Because if he did, you fear he'd leave!)

The Make Every Man Want You approach is completely different. It's about waking up and being alive, being expressive, and, most importantly, being you. It's about healing every false thought you've ever had about love and relationships. It's about discovering your natural ability to be authentic, sensual, and downright irresistible in a way that is true to your soul and inspires others to do the same. Tricks and techniques are cheap. Authentic irresistibility is exquisite. Go for the real deal.

Victimhood Is Prohibited

There are no irresistible victims. Being irresistible means you take full responsibility for your life. That means recognizing that you've engineered your life to be exactly the way it is right now.

Many women believe that the events of their lives are determined by factors that are out of their control. I often hear women speaking of their bad luck in relationships (and in life) as though it was something happening independently of them. They'll say, "Why do I always get guys like this?" or "If I didn't have to work for such a crazy boss, I'd have time to work out and be in shape."

Other women assume their repetitive relationship difficulties stem from a fault within and believe they have some kind of genetic character flaw, again, completely out of their control. They'll say things like, "I can't help myself. I have to be with him. That's just the way I am!" or "I'm just lazy. Getting to the gym is too much work for someone like me." Both are inaccurate.

If you're capable enough to get your hands on a copy of this book, you're capable enough to drop your drama, discover how to be irresistibly you, and do what it takes to have wonderful, satisfying relationships.

Truth Telling Is Required

The women who have the highest success with the Make Every Man Want You approach are the ones willing to tell the truth—to themselves, about themselves. They say, "Yes, I do that!" when they recognize they've been complaining, whining, or behaving in some way that doesn't succeed in producing the results they want (for example, being irresistible or having great relationships with men). They don't beat on themselves or judge themselves for what they discover. They simply notice the truth and move on.

Irresistible women are also willing to let go of their need to be "right" and defend their point of view—as though they know it all already. All true growth and learning comes out of a willingness to not know. Think about it. Whenever you have the courage to say, "I don't know . . ." or "Perhaps there's another way . . . ," you open yourself up for greater insight and possibilities. I always get suspicious when coaching clients quickly say, "Yes, yes, I know that already," when I give them feedback. That snappy "Yes, yes, I know that already" tells me they really don't know that already and are unwilling to look stupid—mostly to themselves. The fact is, what they "know" has gotten them into trouble in the first place. An open, receptive, and nondefensive attitude allows for more expansive, miracle-based relationship possibilities to enter.

We've got to be willing to tell the truth—to ourselves, about ourselves—in order to see and dissolve those things we do to sabotage our relationships. The truth really does set us free.

Humor and Fun Are Strongly Suggested

Right now you're holding a road map to enlightened irresistibility. And as they say, the middle word in enlightenment is *light*. Having a sense of humor about yourself and your past relationship mistakes not only will expedite your results but also will nourish your soul and give you some good laughs along the way.

It takes a level of humility and lightheartedness to see things about yourself that you may consider foolish

Irresistible Action Challenge

What are at least three ways you're already irresistible? Name at least three things you appreciate about you right now.

Bring awareness to how much you say, either in your head or aloud, "I know that already." Can you smile at that thought and gently redirect your attention to hearing or seeing things as though for the first time? How willing are you to be a fresh canvas upon which life can bring you something new?

Lighten up, daaarling. Most of us take ourselves (and our lives) too darn seriously. This unnecessary "tightness" is a real buzz kill to our irresistibility and well-being. Test this for yourself: next time you're getting a little too serious, do a body scan. Are you scrunching up your face or squeezing your shoulders? Notice how you feel. Is it fun? Are you enjoying the experience?

or embarrassing. Be gentle with yourself and recognize there's not a woman on the planet who doesn't have her own personal collection of moments when she said, "What was I thinking?!" when it comes to love and relationships.

Chapter 2

The Five Truths That Every Irresistible Woman Needs to Know

A person does not have to be behind bars to be a prisoner. People can be prisoners of their own concepts and ideas. They can be slaves to their own selves.

—*Prem Rawat, speaker and peace activist*

ou're about to learn five truths that will free you from 99 percent of the relationship drama, frustration, and personal insecurity you've experienced your entire life up until this moment. If you let them, these truths will free you from ever having such experiences again.

As discussed in Chapter 1, many of us are operating on false information. We've been culturally misinformed about what it takes to have and maintain great relationships and, until now, about what it means to be truly irresistible inside and out. When you're operating on false information, you're being misled. You're heading in the wrong direction, and it's impossible to find what you're looking for because you're in the wrong place.

For example, if I told you to bake a cake and gave you the recipe for meatloaf, would you be surprised when your cake tasted like meatloaf? Probably not. If I insisted you had the right recipe for cake and asked you to keep trying, would you ever eventually bake a cake instead of a meatloaf? Nope. That's because when you're operating on wrong information, you're going to keep getting the wrong results. It's no different with men and relationships.

Most of us are operating on wrong information, so it's impossible to experience the kind of loving and satisfying relationships we desire. But as you're about to discover, when you have the right recipe, it becomes easy to have your cake and eat it, too.

TRUTH 1
A Relationship Will Not Save You

> To wait for someone else, or to expect someone else to make my life richer, or fuller, or more satisfying, puts me in a constant state of suspension.
>
> —*Kathleen Tierney Andrews, author*

Many women, including myself, have made the mistake of believing that they need a man or relationship in order to feel complete, whole, less alone, emotionally and/or financially secure, and generally successful in their lives, and it is no wonder. Our culture conditions us to believe we are somehow incomplete or only half of a whole until we are married or in a committed relationship. I call it the Jerry McGuire "you complete me" syndrome. Did you see that movie? In it, Renée Zellweger and Tom Cruise fall in love and profess to one another (in a very teary-eyed and tug-at-your-heartstrings kind of way), "You complete me."

While it's sweet and entertaining in the movies, off the big screen this mentality wreaks havoc on women's (and men's) emotional well-being and ability to actually have a working relationship. Operating from the idea that a relationship (or anything else) will somehow complete you, save you, or make your life magically take off is a surefire way to keep yourself unhappy and unhitched.

Ironically, quite the opposite is true. What you really need to understand is that nothing outside of you can ever produce a lasting sense of completeness, security, or success. There's no man, relationship, job, amount of money, house, car, or anything else that can produce an ongoing sense of happiness, satisfaction, security, and fulfillment in you.

Some women get confused by the word *save*. In this context, what it refers to is the mistaken idea that a relationship will rid you of feelings of emptiness, loneliness, insecurity, or fear that are inherent to every human being. That finding someone to be with will somehow "save" you from yourself. We all need to wake up and recognize that those feelings are a natural part of the human experience. They're not meaningful. They only confirm the fact that we are alive and have a pulse. The real question is, what will you invest in: your insecurity or your irresistibility? The choice is yours.

Once you get that you are complete and whole right now, it's like flipping a switch that will make you more attractive, authentic, and relaxed in any dating situation— instantly. All of the desperate, needy, and clingy vibes that drive men insane will vanish because you've stopped trying to use a relationship to fix yourself. The fact is, you are totally capable of experiencing happiness, satisfaction, and fulfillment right now. All you have to do is start living your life like you count. Like you matter. Like what you do in each moment makes a difference in the world. Because it really does.

That means stop putting off your dreams, waiting for someday, or delaying taking action on those things you know you want for yourself because somewhere deep inside you're hoping that Prince Charming will come along to make it all better. You know what I'm talking about. The tendency to hold back from investing in your career, your health, your home, your finances, or your family because you're single and you figure those things will all get handled once you land "the one."

Psst. Here's a secret: holding back in your life is what's keeping him away.

Don't wait until you find someone. You are someone.

When you live each day with enthusiasm—as though now is all you've got—a funny thing happens. You start to feel happy, satisfied, secure, and fulfilled, pretty much all the time. Rather than just going through the motions and secretly waiting for things to get better once you meet Mr. Right, you start living your life with intensity and, in doing so, awaken that irresistible fox inside you who's been dying to run the show. When you put 100 percent in your life (read: approach everything like it counts), happiness, satisfaction, and *irresistibility* (ding, ding, ding!) are natural by-products. We'll cover exactly what it means to live each day with enthusiasm in Chapter 10 and why it's the ultimate attractant. But for now, just know that despite popular belief, a relationship will not make you any happier, more fulfilled, more satisfied, more financially secure, or more emotionally stable than you are right now.

TRUTH 2
Relationships Are Spiritual Opportunities, Not a Needs Exchange

> Relationship is one of the most powerful tools for growth.
>
> —*Shakti Gawain, author and spiritual teacher*

Many of us have the false idea that a relationship's purpose is to somehow fulfill our needs and desires. We look to see what we can get out of the relationship instead of what we can put in. Looked at like this, relationships are often little more than a needs exchange. We need this (safety, love, intimacy); a man needs that (security, companionship, sex). When we come across a good fit, both parties tacitly agree to do a trade and call it love. This transaction-based relationship model is why so many relationships feel empty and dead. They are completely devoid of anything real and intimate. After the initial rush of excitement is over, they're more like business contracts than sacred unions.

Let's face it. We've all been conditioned to use relationships for the wrong reasons: to end loneliness, relieve depression, recover from a previous breakup, or find security. The problem is that this is not what relationships are for.

Relationships are a spiritual opportunity for personal evolution. There is no greater arena for discovering your capacity for love, forgiveness, compassion, personal greatness, and full self-expression. Nowhere else will you meet the grandest and smallest parts of yourself. Nowhere else will you confront your self-imposed limits to intimacy. Nowhere else can you forgive so deeply or love so purely.

This is relationship's real purpose: to serve the mutual growth and soulful expression of each individual. It's a chance to share your enthusiasm for being alive and give of yourself to another. Relationships provide the opportunity to shed light on any area within you that remains cloaked in fear and uncertainty, to hold a vision of another's greatness so that he may step into the magnificence his soul is yearning to express. In this way, relationship becomes the ultimate tool for personal discovery and spiritual growth.

When we engage in relationship to see what we can put into it rather than what we can get out of it, our whole lives transform. We no longer see our partners as antagonists. We see them as teachers and allies who are here to help us discover and experience our glory.

Does this mean you should stay in an abusive, unhealthy, or otherwise dead-end relationship because you've just discovered relationships are spiritual opportunities to rise above it all and find some greater meaning? Hell no. Remember, it's about mutual growth and soulful expression.

TRUTH 3
*L*ife Is Now—This Is It

> There are only two ways to live your life. One is as though nothing is a miracle. The other is as though everything is a miracle.
>
> —*Albert Einstein*

There were several years when I didn't like the way my life was going. It's not that any part of it was particularly bad. I had steady work, friends, a nice boyfriend, and enough money to pay my rent, shop, and enjoy life in New York City. But there was this constant, nagging feeling inside, and I often thought to myself, "I should be much farther along by now."

At that time I had just started to learn about the benefits of living in the moment. In fact, I often repeated a quote I read in Deepak Chopra's *The Seven Spiritual Laws of Success*, which says, "The past is history, the future is a mystery, and this moment is a gift. That's why it is called the present." But it wasn't until several years later that I really got the full meaning of that expression. It took me a while to understand that this moment—the one right now—*is* really it.

You see, for all those years, I had been living my entire life as though this isn't it.

My job wasn't really it. It was just a day job to pay the bills so I could move on to bigger and better things. No need to stay late or go the extra mile. My relationship wasn't really it. He was just a convenient placeholder till the real Mr. Right showed up. No need to surrender to him and share my heart completely. My apartment wasn't really it. After all, I was renting. No need to decorate or create much of a permanent home.

The "this isn't it" mentality even polluted little things throughout my day; for example, at weddings or special events, I often felt like I was at the wrong table. "This isn't it," I thought. "I should be at the other table." At nightclubs, I often felt like I'd picked the wrong one. "This isn't it," I thought. "The other place is where it's really jumping." At a restaurant, I would think, "This isn't what I wanted. I should've ordered what she did."

For many years, what I failed to realize was that right now is all you ever have. This moment is really it. Rather than fully investing and engaging in my life exactly as it was, I spent most of my time complaining, planning, scheming, hoping, and wishing for things to be different someday. I kept journals, did affirmations, and set goals so that things would get better at some point in the future. Here's the key point I missed: inadvertently, I was training myself to lead a life of mediocrity.

Life is *now*. Life can only be *now*.

Whether you like it or not, this is it. What you have in your life in this very moment—your job, friends, family, and home, the car you drive (or don't drive), the meal you choose, the date you are on (or not on)—all of it is really it. Now, this doesn't mean that things will not change. Everything changes. Life is change. But if you approach your life like this is it, all the time, you'll experience a quantum shift in your reality. You'll be more relaxed, more present, and, inexplicably, more irresistible. Excellence will show up in your life effortlessly.

Hey, you! Yeah, you—the sexy fox reading this book. Write this one down on an index card and carry it with you at all times:

A "this is it" attitude = massive irresistibility.

Women who live moment to moment, like this is it, are naturally and authentically more irresistible than those who don't. Rather than complaining, resisting, whining, or holding back, they are fully engaged, fully alive, and in it to win it in every area of their lives.

Like attracts like. You are much more likely to attract a vibrant, energetic, "this is it" kind of man by being a "this is it" kind of woman.

Irresistible Action Challenge

It's easy to experience "this is it" for yourself. It's like flipping a switch that turns on the light of your irresistibility and illuminates everything you touch. Fully invest in each moment exactly as it is right now. Remember that everything is as it should be. You are a perfect version of you in this moment.

Here are five fun ways to experience "this is it" for yourself:

1. When you order at a restaurant, don't second-guess your choice. Trust whatever you ordered is the perfect thing for you. This is it.

2. At work, rather than wasting time daydreaming, complaining, or wishing you were somewhere else, do

Here's the best part: by practicing "this is it," you'll start to notice dramatic, astonishing shifts in every other area of your life as well. Without trying to make it better, you'll find work more effortless and fun because you won't be wishing you were somewhere else. Your house will look and feel more like a home because you'll be more invested in living there. You'll find yourself less stressed and anxious throughout your day—making you much more alive and energetic.

---

what needs to be done with excellence right now. This is it.

3. On dates, hold aside your judgments and criticisms of the person sitting across from you. Practice simply being there, enjoying yourself and noticing how it feels to be with this person. This is it.

4 At home, take care while you clean, decorate, and tidy up. Make your bed neatly and precisely. Hang pictures with thought and attention. Get the nice towels. This is it.

5. Get dressed, put on makeup, and style your hair like it counts. Take your time and pay attention to the details. This is it.

Practicing "this is it" will also have a powerful impact on your appearance, net worth, and relationships with friends and family. Not bad for one little concept, eh?

TRUTH 4
Men Are As-Is Merchandise, or Love 'Em or Leave 'Em, Baby!

> If the shoe doesn't fit, must we change the foot?
> —*Gloria Steinem*

Have you ever found yourself dating a man and thinking, "He'd be perfect if only he were more affectionate, less controlling, more communicative, less self-absorbed, younger, older, wealthier, more A, less B . . . ?" Chances are, if you've ever dated anyone, you have had these thoughts. Fix-him thinking is rampant in our society and plays a big part in many unhappy relationships. It may also be a mind-set that's keeping you single.

Psst. Here's another secret: men don't want to be changed or improved.

Think about it. Would you feel attracted to a man who constantly tried to change or improve you? Someone who told you to lose a little weight? Wanted you to do a little less talking and more cooking and cleaning? Didn't think so. You've got to give up trying to make him be different than he is if you want to be irresistible. In fact, much of your "wishing he'd be different" keeps him staying exactly the same. (Remember, what we resist persists.)

I've got another question for you. Have you ever been to the "as-is" department at IKEA? It's a big room filled with furniture; small chairs, big tables, couches, entertainment centers, lamps, and assorted pillows fill the space. Some pieces are like new, while others have some wear and tear and require a bit of TLC. All of it is for sale in the condition that you find it, for the price marked.

When you visit the "as-is" department, you look at what's available and choose whether or not you want it. Of course, you can waste time talking to yourself about how you wish something were different . . .

"If that chair were yellow, it would be perfect."
"If that couch were just a little wider, it would work
   for me."
"If that table were a shade darker, it would be ideal for
   my kitchen."

. . . but ultimately you must look at what is and see whether or not it would be a good fit for you right now. If it works, you take it. If not, you move on. Well, guess what? Men are no different. One of the biggest mistakes women make is trying to change or improve a man into something he's not. This includes trying to change the way he feels toward you. Let's repeat this all together, shall we? You cannot change the way a man feels or behaves.

Now don't get me wrong, I'm not saying that men don't change or can't change. People transform their lives all the time. *However*, it is not your job to change or improve anyone—especially your partner. If he wants to change or adjust anything, he needs to choose that on his own.

It's like this. Every human being is a unique and perfect expression of who he or she is in this moment. People can be different than they are right now (this includes you). As an irresistible woman, your job is to simply be here and tell the truth about what works for you and what doesn't. Make is-ness your business and meet life as it shows up—not as you prefer it to show up.

If you don't like something about the man you're dating, you have two choices: (1) communicate in a straightforward yet compassionate way about what doesn't work for you and get his perspective or (2) move on, sista—he's just not the one for you. Communication is essential for any healthy relationship. However, there's a big difference between communicating about what works for you and what doesn't and trying to improve or change someone.

When something doesn't work for you in the relationship, let him know. Tell him what you feel and make it clear you're not blaming him for your feelings. Talk about possible solutions or what does work for you, and *listen* to his response. He may be completely unaware of what he's doing that's upsetting to you and happy to adjust his behavior to support the health of the relationship. On the other hand, he may say, "This is me, honey—take it or leave it!"

Either way, don't blame him for your feelings as though he caused them (because he didn't). When you make your feelings his fault, he'll go into automatic defense mode and not listen to you. The communication lines will be broken, and you'll both feel upset and frustrated. Even if you say you don't blame him for how you feel, if you secretly do blame him, he'll sense your dishonesty and defend himself till he's blue in the face. You'll lose credibility and become instantly unattractive, and he'll dismiss anything accurate and valid you have to say.

Nothing outside of you can ever make you feel something. Those emotions (anger, frustration, upset) live in you. Want proof? Have you ever been happily driving your car when someone wants to cut into your lane and you pleasantly oblige? Now, can you also remember a time when someone cut in front of you and you honked, screamed, and acted like the poster child for road rage? In the latter experience, chances are you were already upset. You had anger and frustration in you, sitting just below the surface. The event itself doesn't cause the upset—it merely is a trigger that justifies what's already happening in you and waiting to get out. So when you blame other people for what you're feeling, you disempower yourself. You're operating from confusion and making yourself the victim of those around you.

Communicate like the brilliant and irresistible woman you are. Refrain from pointing fingers or proving your case by listing all the ways he's done you wrong. Look to see the truth of the situation. Perhaps the disagreement is easily resolvable. Perhaps you can let go of being right about how wrong he is and move on. Or maybe, just maybe, it's an excellent opportunity to get out of an unsatisfying, dead-end relationship.

When a relationship doesn't work out, it doesn't mean there's anything wrong or deficient in either person. It just means that you're not a good fit for one another. It's that simple.

Spiritually, it's selfish to hold on to something that's not working. You're stealing time from him (and yourself) that could be spent in another, more harmonious experience.

The bottom line is this: men don't want to be changed or improved. Allow the both of you to be who you are. Be honest and straight in your communications, but don't try to change, improve, or make him into something he's not.

TRUTH 5
If You Want Guarantees in Love, You Don't Want Love

> For peace of mind, resign as general manager of the universe.
>
> —*Larry Eisenberg, author*

Being authentically irresistible means surrendering to the fact that there are no guarantees in life or love. Life is change. Flowers bloom, then die, then bloom again. The weather knows no rest. The sun rises and sets every day. The tides are forever flowing to and fro. Seasons change. Nothing is permanent. It's the very nature of our universe to be ever expanding, ever shifting, ever growing.

Expecting guarantees in love is unrealistic. Looking for someone to promise or guarantee they're going to love you forever puts an enormous and unrealistic pressure on them (and you) to do something we are all incapable of doing—remaining the same. To fully experience all the glory, adventure, and ecstasy of true love, we've got to be willing to let go of the idea that it can be guaranteed.

Life cannot have guarantees. We never know what lies ahead. All we can do is practice meeting our lives directly, moment to moment, and telling our truth as it shows up. It is in this state of the unknown—in the realm of all possibilities—that your authentic irresistibility lies. It is also the sacred space of pure and authentic love, not the pseudo, pop culture, transaction-based version we are all so desperate to have and hold on to.

When you relinquish trying to control another person, you unchain yourself from the illusion of separateness and the false idea that you are somehow incomplete. Ironically, when you stop trying to control love, you create the space in which it can live and flourish. Oddly enough, you'll feel more secure and complete than you could ever imagine.

Human life is about development and evolution. Relationships are no different.

Rather than looking to see how to hold on to or guarantee you'll have someone's love, show up each day as a person who's willing to be loved. Tell the truth, communicate fully, and support him in becoming the man he wants to be.

Take a look in the mirror. Who are you today? Discover yourself anew. Don't assume you are the same person you were last week or last year. Don't limit yourself with your history. Look at your partner with new eyes each day as well. Who is this person? Rediscover him. Don't assume he is the same person that you were with last week or last year. Don't jail him with your judgments or his past. You cannot control how your partner shows up. What you can

Irresistible Action Challenge

What areas of your life have you unawaredly put on hold? What action steps can you take right now to expand those areas?

For example, if you haven't been investing in your financial health, you could buy a book on personal finances or make an appointment with a financial adviser to get started. If you've been a couch potato lately, you could go for a run or take a yoga class.

control, however, is how you show up in relationship to him. Rather than a stale repetition of the good old days we all fight so hard to re-create, be open to the newness in each moment and give your relationship a chance to breathe.

Trying hard to keep a relationship together is a classic sign that it's falling apart. Don't pretend everything is OK when it's not or gloss over problems in order to save face. Welcome challenges and speak your truth. Every so-called problem is an opportunity in disguise for you to expand and express new levels of your irresistibility.

IIIIIIIIIIIIIIIIIIIII **Irresistible Insight Questions** IIIIIIIIIIIIIIIIIIIII

1. Does something inside you believe you need a partner to be complete? How would your life be different if you were incapable of thinking that thought?

2. How willing are you to shift out of a transaction-based relationship model into a more rich and dynamic model grounded in compassion and mutual growth?

Chapter 3

The Seven Habits of Highly Unattractive Women, or Obstacles to Making Every Man Want You

The best way to break a bad habit is to drop it.

—Leo Aikman, writer and editor

Another name for this chapter could be "Ultimate Man Repellants." These are the ways of behaving that drive men absolutely bonkers. Most (though not all) of these habits are a subset of one life-sucking, attraction-killing misconception—the misconception that a relationship will somehow save or complete you.

Remember, a relationship cannot complete you or bring happiness to your life that you don't have right now. Of course, you can experience tremendous levels of happiness and completion while in a relationship, but it's not because of the relationship.

Don't be discouraged if you have one or several of the habits. Remember, awareness (a judgment-free noticing of anything) is all you need to facilitate resolution.

UNATTRACTIVE HABIT 1
*n*eediness—the Ultimate Man Repellant

When was the last time you heard a guy say, "Guess what? I met this really hot needy chick last night!" Chances are, never. That's because being needy is the ultimate man repellant. If you believe you're incomplete and look to a relationship to solve your problems, that is being needy. Men will pick up on this neediness, and it will effectively repel them.

Here are some classic needy behaviors to look out for:

- Obsessive e-mailing or calling (especially to check and see "if he's OK")
- Compulsive checking of your e-mail or voice mail
- Telling a man that you need him in order to be happy
- Relentlessly saying, "I miss you"
- Making overbearing demands to know exactly where he is and what he's doing 24-7
- Throwing silent or not-so-silent temper tantrums when you don't have his full attention
- Feeling a constant insatiable desire for his approval of how you look and what you're doing

Neediness comes from desperation and is a major turn-off. This habit transcends behavior and is broadcast out like radio waves that men pick up on energetically. So even if you refrain from obsessive calls or compulsively checking e-mail and pretend you've got it all together, he'll sense your true desperate energy and pull away.

Another important point is that neediness puts a tremendous amount of undue pressure on a man. He'll feel a constant demand to perform for you, to be perfect, and/or to match your idealized standard for him . . . or else. If he makes a "mistake," he'll not only have to deal with his own consequences, but he'll feel responsible for your happiness as well.

Also, when you have the false idea that you need him so that you can be happy, you give away all your power. Your well-being is at the constant mercy of another person. You render yourself powerless, and a powerless woman, my dear, is anything *but* irresistible.

UNATTRACTIVE HABIT 2
Incessant Insecurity

"Do I look fat in this?"
"Do you still love me?"
"Do you think she's prettier than me?"
"Am I attractive enough for you?"

Incessant insecurity drives men nuts and feeds your ego illusion that you're somehow deficient and "less than."

When you entertain your insecure thoughts, it's as though you're a bottomless pit that can never be filled no matter how much assurance you receive. That's because the idea that you are less than is false. It's an illusion. An illusion can never be healed because it's not real in the first place.

Insecurity and self-doubt lie within the natural human range of emotions and will never fully disappear. Rest assured that, now and then, everyone on the planet feels pangs of not being "good enough." The key to being irresistible is not to indulge in or entertain those thoughts. But don't resist them either! Simply allow yourself to notice or observe those feelings and say, "Hmm . . . isn't that interesting?" or better yet, "I'm having that thought again . . . so what?" and redirect your attention outward. When insecure thoughts come, allow them to simply pass over your mind like clouds floating across the sky.

Not entertaining insecure thoughts is a learnable skill and an absolute must if you want to be irresistible. It's like this: you can either invest in your self-doubt or invest in your irresistibility. I suggest the latter.

Here's a tip. If you think you look fat in a particular outfit, you probably do. I know that may seem harsh, but it's reality. Not all clothes are meant for all body types. Stick with clothes that you know look fantastic on you and that showcase your assets. Go through your wardrobe with a trusted friend and edit it down so that clothes that have you wondering if you look fat are no longer an option.

Here's another important point. No matter how thin, successful, or attractive you become, insecure thoughts don't go away. That's because you can never resolve an inner false thought with an outer reality. It's like treating the symptom instead of curing the disease. The way to cure the insecurity dis-ease is to allow yourself to feel insecure when you do (in other words, don't resist it). But don't dwell on it either. Instead, shift your attention to what's going on in your environment. That may mean fully listening to a conversation or taking action by organizing your desk. Where your attention goes, energy flows. If you simply notice insecure thoughts without taking them personally or making them mean anything, you'll find they occur much less often. You'll also strengthen your ability to remain present and engaged in your life, which is the key to unleashing your authentic irresistibility.

To be honest, most of our thoughts are pure caca anyway (yes, that's a scientific term). Nothing has meaning other than the meaning we give it. With practice, we can train ourselves not to take our thoughts seriously or personally—especially the nonenlivening ones. When they show up, simply say, "Thanks for sharing," and get on with your life.

UNATTRACTIVE HABIT 3
Clueless Communicator

Women often make communication mistakes that undermine their irresistibility and send men running faster than you can say, "Marriage and kids!"

First of all, most of us don't really listen. What we do is judge whether we like or dislike what a man is saying to us, decide whether we agree or disagree with what he's saying, or determine whether we know it already. We also listen to see if what he is saying fits our agenda (like our agenda to have a boyfriend, get married, or have kids). This is not true listening.

True listening happens when you drop those internal conversations in your mind and simply hear what a man is saying to you from his perspective, as though what he is saying is the most important thing on earth and you need to hear every single word. You don't interpret, analyze, or read into it. You don't say, "In other words . . . ," and go on to put into words what you think he means. You just take it in.

When you truly listen, you become instantly attractive. By really hearing a man, you make him feel special and cared for in a very powerful way. If there's genuine chemistry between you, he'll continue to share more and more of himself because of how open and receptive you are to who he actually is (not who you are trying to get him to be). I cannot emphasize this point enough. If you really want to make every man want you, become a masterful listener.

The second communication mistake that women make is talking about other men in a way that incites jealousy and insecurity in their current partners. Ex-boyfriends, ex-husbands, other people you're dating, and how great your male friends are—all are topics that get sticky and uncomfortable if not handled with care. Here's a hint: if in doubt, leave other men out of your relationship. There is no need to divulge details about your romantic or sexual history or build up other men to instigate competition. Those past images and stories will only haunt your current partner and create a karmic cycle of torturing one another with jealousy-based games.

Third, many women feel the need to talk about things during or after sex as though this is the time to get him to really open up about his true feelings. No, no, no! Pressuring a man to open up during or after sex is not recommended, particularly in the dating stage. Side effects of pressuring men include feelings of frustration, isolation, and, at times, extreme confusion.

It's like this: sex is an incredible opportunity to simply let go and be hot, desirous, and free. It's not about trying to get somewhere or take things to the next level. Making love is about releasing, exploring, and pleasuring yourself and another human being. It is extremely healthy and good for your mind, body, and soul. Think of sex like a form of yoga. At the end of a yoga class, you need to lie back in Savasana (the Corpse pose) in order to soak in all the benefits from the intense postures you performed. You simply lie there in a state of contentment and breathe. It's the same with sex. After you're done, allow yourselves to simply relax and soak up all the healing and rejuvenating energy you created together. If a "next level" conversation evolves naturally, fantastic. But don't force it. Enjoy yourself and how exquisite it feels to simply be with another human being.

UNATTRACTIVE HABIT 4
Sloppy and Unkempt Appearance

Let's be honest, shall we? How you look matters. Yes, men will love you for your caring, affectionate ways, your witty, infectious humor, and your irresistible, devilish charm, but come on now. Give them a chance to experience all your fabulousness by wrapping it in an attractive package!

So many beautiful women let themselves go and wonder why they can't attract a man. If you have packed on the pounds, stopped taking care of yourself, or you think a matching track suit is your dress-up outfit, it's time for a reality check. How you look impacts how you feel. And if you're looking dumpy, chances are you're feeling dumpy, and men are feeling your dumpiness, too. When women get too comfortable in their relationship, they tend to stop trying to look attractive. Some men may be sympathetic for a little while (especially if they are on the same downward spiral), but for many, this lack of caring is the trigger to stray. And it's easy, once you become a couple, to slack off on your appearance. Don't. This includes your personal hygiene (breath, teeth, and, yes . . . down there). While sweaty, post-gym sex can be steamy and dreamy, generally speaking, irresistible women keep themselves clean and fresh.

Commit to taking good care of yourself every day. Pay attention to how you put yourself together. Personally, I'm lucky because my mom was an awesome role model in this department. Even though she spent very little money on expensive clothes or jewelry, she always looked fantastic. She exercised for an hour each day and "made herself pretty," as she called it, by freshening up before my dad got home from work. Her clothes were always neatly pressed and her makeup was applied tastefully with skill and care. Even her cozy morning robe and slippers matched!

The point is this. You don't have to obsess or strive for some unrealistic ideal of perfection. But pay attention and take care of yourself.

UNATTRACTIVE HABIT 5
Hardened and Bitter Attitude

Women who have a hardened and bitter attitude usually take on a certain thin (almost too thin), stern look. They appear stony and tired. It's as though their girlish spirit and soft, womanly charm have been sucked out with a straw. Hardened and bitter women often are very serious about everything and believe that life, especially men, have done them wrong. They may indulge in sarcastic and biting humor, and conversations often morph into complaint fests.

A hardened and bitter attitude is a result of repressed anger. Most of us have been taught that anger is bad and unladylike. We have trouble allowing ourselves to actually experience anger and, therefore, have developed the habit of suppressing it in hopes that it will go away or, at the very least, not be seen. The problem is that suppressing anything doesn't make it disappear. In fact, trying not to feel something is a form of resistance, and because what you resist persists and gets stronger, it's no surprise that suppressed anger leads to a hard and bitter outlook on life.

Thankfully, you don't need years of therapy or anger-management classes to let it go. Simply allow yourself to feel anger when it happens. Experience the emotion. Notice it. Allow it to be there and it will pass. If you've been corking it up for a while, you may feel disproportionately angry when you first practice actually experiencing it. For example, if your boyfriend leaves his towel on the floor again, and you allow yourself to experience how you feel, you may notice a strong desire to blow up and create a huge fight. This is not suggested. Most likely, you've got some old anger (real old, like when-you-were-five-and-someone-took-away-your-lollipop old) that is finally getting a chance to come to the surface. If it's appropriate to express yourself and address the situation, do it. If not, simply experience the sensation of anger and get on with your life.

Here's the good news about being hard and bitter. There's a way to transform it. It's called lightening up. If you have the mistaken idea that life or men have done you wrong, you have cast yourself in the role of victim and need a new part to play. How about this? Try being the star, the heroine, the leading lady in your life. (Much more appealing, don't you think?) Remember, there are no irresistible victims. You can either be an irresistible babe or a hardened and bitter victim. The choice is yours.

UNATTRACTIVE HABIT 6
Catty and Critical

Many women find it challenging to acknowledge and compliment other irresistible women, especially while in the presence of their man. Insecure women will criticize another woman's clothing, shoes, bag, hair, body, makeup, or success. These catty and critical women mistakenly believe that tearing down another, irresistible woman will somehow be a preemptive strike and prevent their man from finding the other woman desirable. Nothing could be farther from the truth!

First of all, being critical of another woman casts you in a bad light. You are seen as insecure and jealous. And let's be honest, your man probably noticed her at least ten minutes before you did, so why pretend otherwise?

Here's the other thing. By bad-mouthing attractive women, you unconsciously program yourself not to become one. The universe is like a big photocopy machine that sends back to you copies of what you "order" through your thoughts. By being catty and critical, your thoughts are sending "attractive is bad" out to the universe, and the universe has no choice but to say, "Yes, master! Attractive is *bad*." Because none of us wants to be bad, we will not allow ourselves to become attractive or, heaven forbid, irresistible.

Here's what to do. When you notice another hot woman, silently bless her and say, "That's right, girl. W-o-r-k!" This will recondition your mind to approve of being attractive, and the universe has no choice but to say, "Yes, master!" and support you in being as foxy as you want to be. Personally, I like to point out attractive women so both my partner and I can enjoy the eye candy. It is fun and supports honesty between us, and the bottom line is that he's coming home with me.

UNATTRACTIVE HABIT 7
Boring in Bed

While no man in his right mind would ever come out and say it, boring sex is a frequent cause of breakups and dead-end relationships. It's not that you have to install a stripper pole in your bedroom or get into hard-core bondage (although either or both could be a lot of fun), but you must investigate your own personal ideas of sexuality and tell yourself the truth about whether or not you hold back in between the sheets. My guess is that on some level, you do. (Let's face it—at times we all do!)

Sex between two consenting adults is a beautiful and revitalizing event. It is one of the most heavenly experiences on earth and can be an incredible expression of intimacy and aliveness. It's also an excellent way to strengthen your irresistibility muscles.

Please repeat this with me out loud. "I love sex. I love sex. I love sex."

Good. Now say this to yourself at least five times a day. Seven more if you were raised Catholic. (Only kidding . . . well, not really.)

Most of us, whether we realize it or not, have been culturally conditioned to believe sex is bad. Even if we say that we like sex, we've been so deeply steeped in a society that considers sex dirty, shameful, and sinful that we often don't feel comfortable talking frankly about it or taking actions to proactively develop our sexual prowess.

A subset of boring sex is doing it just to get it over with. I can think of nothing more unattractive than a woman who lies there mentally reviewing her shopping list or looking at cracks on the ceiling while her man is working up a sweat in an effort to please her. Many women give in so he'll stop asking and then lie there during the act like a dead fish. In case you haven't noticed, this approach does not work if you want to be irresistible and have magical, satisfying relationships.

My suggestion is to practice being naughty and to initiate sex much more frequently. A great way to spice things up is to learn how to striptease. Tons of instructional DVDs are on the market, and live classes are offered in major cities. As a dancer and fitness instructor, I thoroughly enjoy teaching the art of strip. Words cannot describe how invigorating it is to watch women let go of their inhibitions right before my eyes and discover the beauty, elegance, and inner sexpot that resides within. Women truly transform through these classes and feel sexier and more confident than they ever thought possible.

Another great thing to do is to buy beautiful lingerie that makes you look and feel sexy. Get at least one piece that's practical enough to wear under everyday clothes so you can experience a little secret naughty factor all day long.

Last but not least, get practiced receiving pleasure from a man. You can give him no greater gift than allowing him to sexually satisfy you. Many women are not accustomed to simply allowing themselves to receive. You know what? Get over it! If you want to make every man want you, you're going to have to step out of your comfort zone and allow yourself to feel good—really good—on a consistent basis. And don't use the excuse that he doesn't know how to please you. He's not a mind reader, and every woman's body is different. Tell him, show him, guide him. He, and you, will love you for it.

The bottom line is this. Being boring in bed is a function of fear: fear of looking stupid, fear of not knowing what to do, fear of being laughed at, or fear of being flat-out rejected. Irresistible women feel the fear and go for great sex anyway. Remember, practice makes perfect!

Nothing kicks fear in the ass like taking consistent action. When fear-based thoughts come up—and you know they will—say, "Thanks for sharing," and go about being the naughty girl you know you are.

IIIIIIIIIIIIIIIIIIIIII **Irresistible Insight Questions** IIIIIIIIIIIIIIIIIIIIII

1. How often do you check your e-mail or voice mail out of a sense of desperation? How much time are you wasting being needy, in thought or action, that could otherwise be spent enjoying your life?

2. Do you join in when friends are being catty or critical of other irresistible women? Even if you don't, do you stand by in silence or do you speak up and offer a different possibility? Are you willing to support your friends by opening up the door for their irresistible transformation?

Irresistible Action Challenge

Get rid of every single "low self-esteem" item in your wardrobe. You know, those "special" outfits that make you feel dumpy, frumpy, and at least ten pounds heavier the second you put them on. This is a great challenge to do with friends.

Practice true listening. Notice how often you finish people's sentences (in your head or aloud)—and cut it out. Pretend the person who's speaking has a gem of wisdom to tell you that will profoundly change your life. But in order to receive it, you have to give the person your full attention and allow him or her to speak without interrupting. Assume the person may need to ramble a bit at first in order to get to the really good stuff later.

Do you let your appearance fall to the back burner? Schedule your manicures, pedicures, facials, and hair appointments for the next six months.

It's time to get your sexy back. And there's no better way than by having an entertaining naughty buffet. (This can be done alone or with a partner.) Rent adult movies and read an erotic or trashy romance novel. Notice what gets your motor running. Have fun breathing life into your sensual side.

Part 2

Eight Secrets to Magnetizing Men

Trust that still, small voice inside that says,
"This might work and I'll try it."

—*Diane Mariechild, author*

Chapter 4

SECRET 1

To Hell with the Rules

The golden rule is that there are no golden rules.

—*George Bernard Shaw*

I have to say it. I hate rules. They're so damn confining. Not to mention they don't work, especially when it comes to relationships.

When you apply a rule, which is a decision you made about something in the past (usually during an upsetting moment), you pollute the present moment and close down an infinite number of possibilities. You contaminate your future with often inaccurate and obsolete information based on past events. Every moment is new and brilliantly unique because it's never happened before. Ever.

Dating rules and techniques are designed out of fear and scarcity. They exist to keep your partner off-balance so he has to keep wondering about you and put his attention on you rather than on living the fullness of his own life. You do not want this. This is not true love; it's a never-ending game of manipulation.

Rules Kill Your Irresistibility

Our universe is forever expanding. That includes you. I'm certain you are smarter, more experienced, and more centered than you were ten years ago. Basing your approach to love on rules that may, or may not, have worked for you in the past (even if the past is twenty minutes ago) is like following a road map to a destination that no longer exists. When you follow rules for love, you kill your irresistibility and aliveness. There is no creativity in rules—no room for new possibilities or something wonderful to be born from the unknown.

Rules are often someone else's truth that you've adopted as your own. Many women have unconsciously absorbed other people's rules from their religion, their family, or the media. Others pick up self-help material that encourages manipulation and find it easier to follow some system rather than looking to discover their own truth.

Here are some common dating rules that wreak havoc on authentic irresistibility:

- Never call a man.
- Don't make eye contact with men.

- Don't talk too much.
- Don't have sex on the first date.
- Never date more than one man at a time.
- Don't make the first move.
- Don't invite a man up to your place.
- Never date a man who is shorter than you.

I say, rules shmules!

There are times when calling a man is absolutely the thing to do. Eye contact can be very sexy. Talking can be soul enlivening. Sex on the first date can lead to an intensely satisfying lifelong relationship. Dating several men can be fun and exciting.

Now there are times when these behaviors don't work and do kill your irresistibility. It's not, however, because of the "rule." It's because of who you are being when you're calling, looking, sexing, dating, and so on. You can break every rule in the book when you are fully centered and self-aware because you're in touch with your irresistibility.

Who You Are Being Makes All the Difference

Who you are being makes all the difference in the world when it comes to authentic irresistibility. Let me say this again for emphasis because it's the most important concept in the entire book:

Who you are *being* makes all the difference in the world when it comes to authentic irresistibility.

If you're being needy (see Unattractive Habit 1, Chapter 3) when you call men because you don't yet realize a relationship will not save you (see Truth 1, Chapter 2), you will effectively repel men.

If you're having sex with a man because you think it will make him love you and want to be with you, you've failed to understand that you cannot change the way a man feels (Truth 4, Chapter 2) and you'll find yourself disappointed and feeling used (ironically, not because he used you but because you used yourself to try to manipulate another human being).

If you want to get married and have a family because you think it will guarantee he'll love you forever or you'll finally get the financial security you've dreamed of, you missed that if you want guarantees in love, you don't want love (Truth 5, Chapter 2), and that relationships are spiritual opportunities, not a needs exchange (Truth 2, Chapter 2).

Want more? Let's say you use rules or techniques to land your man. You've followed every step in the system and caught him with a strategic set of manipulative games. What happens then?

In order to keep him, you'll have to maintain that charade for the rest of your life. You'll have to lie incessantly about what works and what doesn't in order to abide by the "rules." You'll never be able to fully and authentically express yourself or give and receive unconditional love, because that's not part of the big calculated game plan to keep him on his toes.

Relationships produced from rules require constant and exhausting self-management and overall self-deadening. My suggestion? To hell with the rules!

Manipulation never produces deeply intimate love or satisfying relationships. True and lasting love springs from authenticity, communication, and a willingness to fully surrender to another human being.

You don't need rules. You need truth. Your truth. His truth. Your collective truth—communicated to each other in a spirit of respect and compassion, free from finger-pointing, blame, and manipulation. I can think of nothing sexier than a woman who is unashamedly herself—honest about her feelings, authentic in her expressions, and secure enough to share her insecurities as they come up.

It is in the realm of limitless possibilities, not rules, that true love lives. Through straightforwardness, not manipulation, magnificent relationships are born. And it is out of integrity, authenticity, and self-respect that your irresistibility will flourish.

Irresistible Action Challenge

What rules have you abided by up until now? Write them down.

Now consider these questions. Where did you learn the rules you wrote down? Are they working for you? How willing are you to break free from the old mold of "rules" and step into the world of limitless possibilities?

Chapter 5

SECRET 2
Trash Your Perfect
Man Checklist

> If you judge people you have no time to
> love them.
>
> —*Mother Teresa*

About five years ago, I had a type—my own perfect man checklist, if you will: not so tall, Italian (or Italian-esque), Catholic, within about three years of my age, never married, no kids (nor did he want any), and having a certain amount of . . . um . . . Jersey-ness. He was preferably a smart, savvy, suit-wearing kind of man (not some artistic, creative type). I couldn't even conceive of being with someone who didn't fit that profile. Mind you, it's not as though I thought to create this date-ability criteria. It was unconsciously put together from things I saw growing up in the family and culture I grew up in.

My perfect man checklist was blown to bits when I started living my life directly and began investigating the way I operated, just like you are doing here. It was really exciting for me. I discovered that whole new worlds of men existed out there. Much to my surprise (and his), I fell deeply in love with a man named Josh, a Jewish actor-writer-director several years older than I, who was divorced with a nine-year-old son.

Ha! Almost the exact opposite of what I thought would make me happy. Almost the complete reverse of my perfect man checklist.

I tell you from experience: what I know now to be possible in terms of love, partnership, and intimacy is far beyond what I could have ever imagined before meeting him. My ideas of the perfect man were so small, so limited—downright pale in comparison to the reality and brilliance I experience with Josh on a daily basis.

What it took for me to discover my truth (and Josh) was a willingness to fully let go of my ideas of what I thought would make me happy and to allow something new and utterly unknown to enter in. Prior to meeting him, my mind was so filled up with old thoughts, judgments, restrictions, and perfect man criteria, I was unable to even see that anything else existed.

Using a perfect man checklist makes it nearly impossible to attract the right man for you. Your ideas of perfect are narrow and limiting. They come from what you already know, which means they are derived from the past—from a less expansive, less experienced, less irresistible version of you.

Your perfect man checklist, whether it's a list you have consciously compiled or one you subconsciously absorbed from your culture, is cutting you off from boatloads of loving and available men. The perfect man checklist acts as a restrictive filter—sifting, sorting, and screening who you'll even consider dating. It's a self-imposed barrier to love and holds many women back from the possibility of having a magical relationship. Your checklist has probably even turned into a mental fantasy of someone I like to call . . .

The Mythical Mr. Right

You know this guy. He's the idealized picture you have of the person you should be with for the rest of your life. Of course, no mortal man can hope to compete. He's mythical because he's based on a story of who you think will make you happy. He's fictional—a fantasy composite you've dreamed up based on limited and narrow information from your past. He's a made-up man in your mind, not a real man in your bed.

I ask you this: what if your current image is shortsighted? What if there's someone out there with incredibly wonderful qualities you can't even imagine yet? What if you're more invested in your fantasy than in reality? What if within nanoseconds of meeting someone you unconsciously compare him to your mythical Mr. Right and conveniently judge him as not "the one" so you can avoid the challenge and intimacy of a real relationship?

Are you willing to let go of what you *think* will make you happy in order to discover something more exciting, more intimate, and more loving than you could ever imagine? Are you courageous enough to have a real relationship with a real man?

What if the idea of Mr. Right is completely false? What if there is no Mr. Wrong? What if every relationship—no matter how brief—contains a priceless lesson allowing you to grow and evolve into your grandest self?

Irresistible Action Challenge

Write out your perfect man checklist and list all of the character traits of your mythical Mr. Right. This includes all of the ways you sort, sift, and screen potential partners. Some ideas to get you started are his hair color, height, ethnicity, age, occupation, and income. Is there any type you won't date or even consider giving a second look?

Done? Good. Now burn the list.

One last thing. You are a goddess, a queen. You know so much more than you think you do, and it does not come from your mind. It is born from your spirit—from your inner knowing, your higher self, the divine intelligence within you. You are intuitive, perceptive, and wise.

In order to unleash your authentic irresistibility, you've got to be willing to step outside the confines of your mind and open yourself up to the limitless possibilities of the universe. Rest assured that opening up your possibilities does not mean that the man you fall in love with won't have qualities you desire. It just means that you stop living out of old, self-limiting ideas and thoughts and discover what's true for you now.

Why restrict yourself to some made-up idea of who you think you should be with? What if someone beyond your wildest dreams is just around the corner waiting for you if you are open enough to see him? Why put up barriers to love?

Irresistible Action Challenge

Let go of finding Mr. Right and simply start having fun. (What a concept!) Say this three times aloud right now:

I date for *fun*, not to find the one!
I date for *fun*, not to find the one!
I date for *fun*, not to find the one!

Stop putting so much pressure on yourself and on the men you date. Reawaken your girlish spirit and enjoy yourself again. Play. Laugh. Be silly. Have an adventure on dates. What do you have to lose besides your singleness? Trust your intuition. If you feel attracted to someone who's not "your type," go out with him anyway and open yourself up to new possibilities.

You never know whom you might discover.

Chapter 6

SECRET 3
When It's Men vs. Women, Everyone Loses

Know that you cannot help but judge. What you then do with your judgment is the choice.

—*Story Waters, author and spiritual teacher*

*M*ost of us have heard the phrase *battle of the sexes*. It refers to the fact that most men and women are in a constant power struggle to outdo one another. Men are trying to prove their superiority over women while women are doing the same. Despite the social and political advances of women over the past century, this gender war still exists in our society and, left unexamined, damages your ability to attract men as well as to maintain and enjoy healthy relationships with them.

This rivalry of men versus women has been culturally passed down from generation to generation since the beginning of time. And all of us, whether we recognize it or not, have been deeply influenced by it. Until you become fully aware of all the nuances of its existence, you unwittingly participate in this war and are destined to keep behaving in ways that erode your irresistibility. This unexamined contempt for men will pop up and sabotage an otherwise healthy relationship.

Here's what happens. Day in and day out you absorb messages (consciously and unconsciously) that reinforce the gender war. In magazine articles, TV shows, and casual conversations, we are bombarded with statistics, stories, and remarks to prove one gender is outsmarting, outearning, or outliving the other. Even friends and family often influence and reenroll you in the fight against men. You'll engage in male-bashing joke fests or multihour complaint calls with the girls about how insensitive, uncommunicative, untrustworthy, self-centered, lazy, and noncommittal all men are. Aunt Sally will say, "Oh, dear, there's nothing you can do—all men are like that." Or your best friend will say, "You know men—they just don't get it." Deep inside, you, too, feel somehow wronged by men and may say or do things (intentionally or not) that leave the men you spend time with feeling defensive, slighted, or inadequate.

Many single women I know have a habit of systematically emasculating men and then wonder why they're alone or in a combative relationship. Let's take my client

Ali's story as an example of everyday innocent conversation that reenrolled her in the gender war.

li's Story

Ali is a thirty-one-year-old publicist in the fashion industry. She's blonde, attractive, and financially successful. She has had several relationships that all ended badly and is eager to settle down and start a family. She recently started dating Mike, a high-powered business analyst. After a few weeks dating Mike, Ali had the following conversation with her friend Sharon.

Ali: "You know, Mike called to cancel our dinner plans tonight because he has a big project due at work tomorrow. He told me he'd take me out on Friday night instead, but I'm still disappointed."

Sharon: "That's such a guy thing. Men are just so inconsiderate—all they care about is themselves."

Ali: "You think they're all like that?"

Sharon: "Of course they are. And it gets worse once you move in together. Do you think my Gary ever helps clean up our apartment? God forbid I ask him to make the bed or take out the trash. He'd rather sit his fat ass on the couch all day and watch TV. Men!"

Can you see how a seemingly innocent conversation can enroll you in the gender war? Most likely, Ali will punish Mike by withholding sex and acting slightly distant, hoping that he gets the point that she's upset about something. This approach is not recommended! If you want to be irresistible and have magical relationships, you've got to stop looking at men like they are a different species, out to do you wrong. This attitude is no different from racial or religious discrimination. Start looking at men and women as unique and individual people.

Many women ask, "Where are all the real men?" or complain, "There just aren't enough single men my age. They all want younger women." Women who make remarks like these fail to see, unbeknownst to themselves, that they harbor a deep-seated contempt for men. They unconsciously look for ways to prove men do it wrong, think wrong, behave wrong, and are wrong. It's impossible to attract a loving and satisfying relationship with a man, and have it last, if you are a secret or not-so-secret man hater.

Here are some tendencies to watch out for:

- You compete with men professionally to prove women are better.
- You look for ways to prove women have it harder.
- You make or laugh at male-bashing jokes.
- You hold resentments, judgments, or complaints against your father.
- You spend more time complaining about men than actually dating them.

*Y*our Thoughts About Men Affect the Way They Behave Toward You

Another interesting aspect of the gender war that most women forget is that their thoughts and judgments about men impact the way men behave around them. If you believe your thoughts reside exclusively in the privacy of your mind, think again. Your thoughts are palpable and resonate with others. If you judge someone as incompetent, insensitive, or stupid, they feel it. This includes men.

Some people are more skillful at noticing and naming this type of energy, but everyone is affected by it. Whether you like it or not, you have an impact on how people, especially men, behave around you. Your ideas, thoughts, and beliefs about people influence how they treat you. Perception is an act of creation. Thinking all men are generally stupid, untrustworthy, insensitive, or chauvinistic will actually push them to behave in those ways toward you. It's as though you are nudging them in that direction and then get to say, "See! Look—I'm right. All men do suck."

In his groundbreaking book *The Hidden Messages in Water*, Dr. Masaru Emoto scientifically proves that thoughts and feelings affect physical reality. He tested different focused intentions on frozen water molecules. He discovered that the frozen water labeled with loving thoughts like "gratitude" and "thank you" and "I love you" had beautiful, symmetrical, complex snowflakelike molecul

Irresistible Action Challenge

Quit doing battle with men by seeking out all the ways you may engage in it. Until you bring awareness to how it happens, it's impossible to stop. Use the following questions to support you:

1. Do you allow male bashing in your presence? Even if you don't participate, being around that type of commentary brings down your energy and affects your irresistibility. Start speaking up, or remove yourself from gender-biased complaint fests.

2. What thoughts or beliefs about "all men" do you hold as the truth? Write them down. Are they supportive or destructive to your irresistibility? Are you willing to see that these are just old thoughts that may not be yours? Can you let them go?

3. How willing are you to make a difference in the world by sharing your insight with friends and family when a gender-biased conversation comes up? Can you do it in a way that doesn't make anyone wrong but merely points out the futility of gender-biased beliefs?

terns with vibrant color tones. In contrast, water exposed to negative thoughts like "I hate you" and "you make me sick" had incomplete, distorted, asymmetrical molecular patterns with dull and muddy colors.

When you consider that nearly 75 percent of the human body is composed of water, it's not hard to see that having thoughts like "All men suck" or "I hate men" may not exactly be supporting your irresistibility.

Chapter 7

SECRET 4

Your Parents Didn't Screw You Up (and Even if They Did . . .)

We are disturbed not by what happens to us,
but by our thoughts about what happens.

—*Epictetus, Greek philosopher*

*W*e live in a society that is conditioned to blame the state of our lives on what our parents did or didn't do to us growing up. Either your parents were around too much and controlled and smothered you or they weren't around enough and left you with "commitment issues."

One of my biggest breakthroughs, which completely transformed my irresistibility and my ability to have a successful relationship, was really understanding that my parents didn't screw me up. Until my midtwenties, I believed I had a dysfunctional family and mildly abusive childhood. I was completely comfortable blaming my own inadequacies and failed relationships on my parents.

I would tell men I dated "poor me" stories about how bad my mother was and how she screwed me up. I dubbed her a neurotic "clean freak" and held resentments against her for constantly making me pick up after myself. While I didn't have as many stories about my dad, I nevertheless thought he worked too much and I silently begrudged him for failing to save me from my mother's mean ways.

Can you say, "What a total crock!"

My childhood was neither dysfunctional nor mildly abusive. The only dysfunction that occurred was in my bratty little mind. I told those "poor me" stories based on memories I put together as a difficult, hormone-crazed teenybopper who did not like to be told what to do. (Very much like lots of other teenyboppers on the planet.)

I had no awareness of how challenging it is to be a parent or the complexities and demands that come along with caring for and raising a family. Like many children, I was untidy and self-absorbed and I needed discipline. Looking back with my adult eyes, I'm 100 percent certain I did things that drove my parents nuts! There's no doubt I left the bathroom a sticky, hairspray-coated mess and my bedroom looking like it had been hit by a tornado. The memories of my childhood as dysfunctional are not at all accurate. They were recorded in my mind by a much younger version of me—during a time I was upset and having a temper tantrum. I had a child's perspective, which, by its very nature, is limited and incomplete. I recorded my mom's very normal and responsible parenting as somehow dysfunctional or abusive. Until I brought awareness to it, I brought that story with me forward in time as though it were true—limiting my own irresistibility and capacity for a full, mature, and satisfying relationship with a man.

In reality, my mother is incredibly loving, wildly supportive, and a true angel in my life. Thank God she raised me as she did. Who knows what kind of trouble I would have gotten myself into otherwise? And regarding her "neurotic cleaning," she is a true domestic goddess; thankfully, I inherited her enthusiasm for having things around me neat and well taken care of.

And thanks to my father's entrepreneurial success (what I dubbed "working too much"), financially we had everything we could have ever wanted and more. And as far as quality time goes, we went on countless family vacations, took day trips on the weekends, and spent every holiday together. My father never missed attending a special event throughout my entire life. Also, to his credit, he passed along his ambitious spirit and powerful work ethic, which have fueled my career and the very creation of the book you have in your hands right now.

If you're holding on to a story that your parents screwed you up, you severely limit what's possible for you in terms of love and relationship. You squash your irresistibility because you are not yet behaving as a full, adult woman. Instead of being an authentic, unique individual, you're stuck being not like your parents. Rather than living an expansive life based on discovering your truth, you're living life in reaction to your parents—proving how much they allegedly screwed you up by staying right below the edge of successful or choosing to date bad boys purely to piss them off.

All of this drama is eroding your well-being and preventing you from having the loving and satisfying relationships with men (and your parents) that you deserve.

Here's the other thing. Like it or not, our parents are our archetypal images of men and women. In other words, our mother is our primary image of a woman and our father is our primary image of a man. If we, as women, have the idea that our mothers raised us wrong, should have done it better, or were "mean" moms, we will unconsciously sabotage ourselves. Think about it. How can we fully grow into our own womanhood and irresistibility if our primary image of a woman is flawed? We'll have to prove we're flawed as well by continuing to fall short in life.

If we have the idea that our fathers raised us wrong, should have done it better, or were "bad" dads, we will continue to project that defective masculine image onto every man we meet. It makes no difference whether the man is a friend, a boss, an employee, or a lover. You will unconsciously assume that he is somehow out to hurt or damage you or that, simply because of his gender, he cannot be trusted.

Again, despite popular belief, you do not need years of therapy to heal these issues. All you need are awareness and compassion. Investigate your inner landscape and see if you're carrying around old grievances. Notice what's there and don't judge yourself for what you discover. See what is without diving into a story about what is. True awareness is enough to facilitate resolution. Really. (Didn't I tell you this was going to be easy?)

And Even if They Did . . .

Now what if you actually did have a dysfunctional childhood? What if you were abused? I am by no means suggesting that you made up or inaccurately recorded your abuse. Tragic and unfortunate things do happen. What I am suggesting is that you investigate how holding on to the story of your abuse impacts you now. Is it keeping you from dating? Are you dragging a story from the past into your present and allowing it to keep you from the experience of love and intimacy you deserve?

Oprah Winfrey is a survivor of childhood abuse. In case you haven't noticed, there's nothing that can stop that irresistible woman. And Oprah, as astonishing as she is, is just a woman like you and me. If she can do it, we can, too.

Oprah was willing to let go of her story about her past so that her true irresistibility could heal the world. There are millions of other not-so-famous women who have survived dysfunction and abuse as well and have discovered the freedom that comes with releasing the past. The way out is through forgiveness, of both yourself and anyone else you might still resent for some wrongdoing. Each moment, the universe provides us with a clean slate upon which we can start anew. Take it and use it. The past is over. It's done. The only way it can continue to haunt you is if you allow it to do so.

⸿⸿⸿⸿⸿⸿⸿⸿⸿⸿ Irresistible Insight Questions ⸿⸿⸿⸿⸿⸿⸿⸿⸿⸿

1. Are you holding on to grievances against your parents from childhood? How much time do you spend reliving the past? What impact does it have on your aliveness? On your irresistibility?

2. Is holding on to the story of your childhood serving you? Is it supporting your aliveness? Do you have the relationship of your dreams?

Irresistible Action Challenge

Write down any "poor me" stories about your childhood that you're holding on to. Ask yourself if they are accurate. Is it possible that your memories are skewed? Have you considered how challenging it is to raise a family? Put food on the table? Manage a household, career, and bratty kids?

Even if your story is factual, the important question for you is, now what? Are you willing to let go of the past in order to allow your irresistibility to fully blossom? What gifts are you stealing from the world by remaining entrenched in your past?

Are you willing to let go of the idea that your parents raised you wrong? Are you willing to be a wildly successful, expansive, and irresistible woman?

Chapter 8

SECRET 5

Drop Your Story

The truth you believe and cling to makes you
unavailable to hear anything new.

—Pema Chödrön, author and Buddhist nun

very woman has a story about her life. Your story
is your personal history, as you remember it, from
the moment you were born up to this very moment now. It
includes all of the details of your childhood, your family,
and where you went to school and, most importantly, the
reasons you have come up with to explain why you are the
way you are today. It includes all the things about others
that you believe to be the truth.

We all need to recognize that our stories are based in
the past and often disrupt our relationships and, of course,
our irresistibility. Let's take a closer look and see how.

When a man asks you to tell him a little something about yourself, your personal story is usually what comes out. It often includes the basic facts like your age, your ethnicity, your education, your political ideology, and your religion or spiritual beliefs. Your story also includes your personal shortcomings and the various ways you label yourself, like "I'm not pretty/tall/thin/interesting/young enough" or "Men just don't find me attractive" or "I'm a strong, independent woman," or "I'm too sensitive." Here are some more stories we tell:

- I'm bad in relationships.
- I'm not a good cook.
- I'm introverted.
- I'm bad with money.
- I'm talkative.
- I'm unattractive.
- I'm shy.
- I'm lazy.
- I'm too old.
- I'm too young.

When you drag your story into this moment, a few things happen. First, you pollute your present with the past. You contaminate the freshness impregnated in every moment and limit your potential and—yep, you got it!—your irresistibility. Second, you may also be telling a tall tale that's not even true. For example, in seventh grade your teacher may have said, "You're too tall, Jen. Stand in the back so others can see." It's quite possible that, at thirteen years old, you may have been big for your age. However, as an adult, you may not be. And even if you are tall as an adult, by putting your tall story in front of the fact that, first and foremost, you are a human being, you encourage everyone (especially men) to focus on that which you focus on and consider a shortcoming.

Third, you get stuck in a self-fulfilling prophecy because you believe your story and disregard any information that doesn't support your perspective. It's like you have blinders on and will only gather evidence that proves your story true and will completely dismiss anything that suggests otherwise. For example, if you hold on to a story that all men cheat, you will effectively filter out any information that proves to the contrary. While watching a TV show, you may notice a man cheating on a woman and say to yourself, "See, they all do it." Without realizing it, you'll completely dismiss examples of faithful men because that information doesn't support your perspective.

Similarly, if you hold on to a story that men don't find you attractive, you'll miss noticing subtle romantic advances or displays of interest from men. While out with friends, you may be talking with a man and be completely unaware that he's interested in dating you because it's counter to your "I'm so unattractive" story. Let's take a look at how one woman's story instantly destroyed her irresistibility.

From a Perfect 10 to a Perfect Nightmare

Ronnie is forty-two and single. He has a fiery personality, a strong athletic body, tan skin, and deep, dark eyes. One evening at a swanky lounge in downtown NYC, he met Sheila, a stunning brunette with dark eyes and a killer body—what many would consider a perfect 10. Sheila and Ronnie hit it off immediately. They danced and felt an undeniable attraction for one another. After about twenty minutes of casual flirting and fun, Ronnie glanced at his watch and realized it was much later than he had thought. He needed to get back to Brooklyn to walk his dog.

Disappointed, Ronnie told Sheila he had to leave but he'd love to see her again. To his delight, she, too, lived in Brooklyn and offered to join him on the late-night dog walk. Ronnie was ecstatic. This beautiful woman he had just met was actually going home with him to walk his dog!

Ronnie and Sheila closed out their tab at the bar and jumped in a taxi. Ronnie was psyched. "She's so great," he thought. "Sweet, gorgeous, lives nearby, and likes dogs." He had been single for a while and was excited at the possibility of a new relationship. What happened next was shocking.

During their cab ride to Ronnie's place, Sheila began to tell him her story. From her troubled childhood to her laundry list of not-so-nice ex-boyfriends, Sheila systematically told Ronnie every sordid detail from her past in hopes of creating an instant, personal connection with him. Between horror stories, she managed to squeeze in how unattractive she felt and repeatedly solicited Ronnie's opinion of how she looked.

Ronnie, initially overjoyed about "a perfect 10" coming home with him was now scrambling to figure out how to get as far away from her as possible. He couldn't believe that such a beautiful woman could become so downright nauseating in a matter of minutes. Things got worse. As soon as they arrived at Ronnie's apartment, Sheila insinuated that she wanted to have sex. Ronnie felt bad and uncomfortable. He was so turned off by her stories that he turned her down and politely asked her to leave.

"It was unbelievable," he said. "This absolutely stunning woman became the biggest turnoff I'd ever seen in a matter of minutes. I had *zero* interest in having sex or ever seeing her again because of how much baggage she has."

Bottom line? Unleash your irresistibility by dropping your story. That includes your history (ex-boyfriends, ex-husbands, ex-childhood) as well as self-limiting ideas you tell yourself (you know—that you're not very attractive, you're not good enough, and so on).

If you're a chronic storyteller, practice letting that go and notice what's happening in your environment. Talk about the food, the decor, music, mutual friends, movies, or current events. Share what you're passionate about. Let men experience who you are now as opposed to your well-rehearsed story of your past. When you do talk about your past, do it from a place of self-awareness. Don't victimize yourself or recount tragic events as though they mean something (because they don't). Realize that every experience you ever had has brought you to this moment and has served your own personal and spiritual evolution. The past is gone. Dead. Done. Your life is now. When you drop your story and allow yourself to simply be who you are right now, you instantly become more alive, more engaged, and—all together now—"more irresistible."

One important note: dropping your story does not mean you can't talk about the past. Just become aware of how you do it. Don't complain, whine, or victimize yourself. Express who you are in a way that is free from drama and blame.

Irresistible Action Challenge

What's your story? List the ideas, beliefs, and theories you have put together over time that, up until reading this chapter, you believed to be true.

Now take a look. Is it possible you've been telling yourself a tall tale? How about stories like Sheila's? Do you have a set of past grievances you trot out to prove how much you've overcome or how hard you've had it in hopes of creating intimacy or admiration from a man? How irresistible would you be if you left the past alone? How much more authentic and grounded would you feel? Without your story, how much easier will you make it for a man to really, genuinely want you?

Chapter 9

SECRET 6

Quit Complaining and Start Engaging, or How and Where to Meet More Men than You Can Shake a Stick At

What you are aware of you are in control of;
what you are not aware of is in control of you.

—*Anthony De Mello, Jesuit preist and author*

Have you ever noticed how much time you waste complaining (either aloud or in the privacy of your thoughts) that either you're too busy or you don't know where to meet more men? Here's a big secret: you miss opportunities every single day to meet quality men and you don't even know it.

There's a law in physics that no two things can occupy the same space at the same time. In other words, either you can be complaining about your life and how you have no time to meet men or you can be living your life and meeting men. You cannot do both at the same time.

When you are consumed with the conversation in your mind about what's wrong in life, your irresistibility level takes a noticeable nosedive. It doesn't matter what you complain about: the weather, traffic, your job, a bad hair day, men, women, your parents, the president—any subject matter will do, and all have the same tragic effect.

Here's what happens. When you complain internally, you are lost in thought. When you're lost in thought, you miss what's happening in your environment. Rather than having your attention outward to see who's around and what's going on, you are preoccupied with your internal mental conversation (read: "complaint fest") and miss countless opportunities to meet men.

Energetically speaking, when you are lost in your thoughts, you are a closed system that's emitting "I'm not available" vibes. You reduce the probability of meeting someone because spiritually, you're not open for business.

Why You Should Drop Your Drama

Complaining, whether silently or aloud, is a major man repellant. When you complain, you are arguing with what is; you're saying life is not how you think it should be. This victimizes you and creates stress and anxiety in your body. And that stress has a negative impact on your appearance: premature aging, a worsening of acne or psoriasis, and, my personal favorite, an increase in cortisol, the stress hormone that causes an increase in abdominal fat.

That being said, men are attracted to more than looks in a woman. They are attracted to the way you make them feel. Women who are complaint-free make men feel good because they themselves feel good.

How to Meet More Men Now

Want to know the easiest way to meet more men? Quit complaining and start engaging. That's right. You can meet more men *everywhere*, starting today. It's your attitude that matters most. Rather than having a private pity party, practice redirecting your attention outward and start connecting with everyone in your environment, just for fun. It doesn't matter if they are men or women, young or old, married or single—simply start relating to people instead of being lost in your thoughts. Mail carriers, bankers, grocers, people behind the counter at Starbucks, fellow gym members, cops, teachers, and people in the crosswalk are all fair game.

Don't worry about what to say. A simple hello and a smile are all you need. Take the attention off yourself (and your internal complaints), and redirect your irresistible energy out into the world. Make someone's day by smiling for no reason. Be of service. Kindly hold a door, offer a seat, or lend a hand. Silently bless people around you. You'll be shocked at what happens. You'll start meeting people all the time and feel dramatically more energetic and alive. Synchronistic events will happen more frequently. You'll be in tune with the universe and notice that life flows much more easily.

When you take the attention off yourself and your internal dialogue, people take notice. Casual encounters often turn into friendships, business connections, or even dates. You'll naturally become a better communicator and feel inexplicably more pleasant and relaxed.

Make it a habit to consistently engage with your environment rather than getting caught in an isolated mental loop of complaint. Keep bringing your attention back to what is happening right now, and you'll train yourself to be both expressive and alive—two qualities that are naturally irresistible. This is known as the art of full engagement. Full engagement means bringing your total presence—mental, emotional, physical, and spiritual energy—to whatever it is that you're doing. It doesn't matter if you're standing in line at the bank or hosting a dinner party; engage the fullness of your attention and intention. It means to live in the moment, not in your head. Think *participation*. Think being a "Yes!" Rather than wasting time lost in your thoughts, live your life with full-blown awareness and enthusiasm. When someone asks for a volunteer, raise your hand. When music comes on, dance. When the dishes need to be done, wash them.

The secret to lasting irresistibility is to build a habit of being fully engaged, moment to moment, in everything you do. You can't pretend to be fully engaged as a manipulation to try to produce a date or meet more men. It has to be authentic. Practice for the simple joy and satisfaction that comes from being fully awake and enthusiastically involved in your life.

Being authentically irresistible is about being alive and engaged. The easiest way to do that is to stay out of your head and in your life. Talk with people regardless of their date-ability. Connect with everyone—animals, plants, old ladies, little babies. Share yourself. Be wherever you are with totality.

‖‖‖‖‖‖‖‖‖‖‖ Irresistible Insight Questions ‖‖‖‖‖‖‖‖‖‖‖

1. Do you often complain about things you have absolutely no control over, like the weather and traffic? Does it help?

2. Are you willing to look and see how much of your life is currently wasted on complaints? How many more men would you meet if you took your attention off your complaints and redirected it out in your environment?

3. What other kinds of relationships might you develop? Friendships, business contacts?

Irresistible Action Challenge

Become a complaint-free zone for a day. This game is a fun way to bring awareness to how much of your life you spend complaining. You can play by yourself or with friends. For one full day, don't complain about anything. That includes the weather, your body, men, work, coworkers, politics, or money. Anytime you catch yourself complaining mentally or out loud, just drop it.

Chapter 10

SECRET 7

Get a Life and Keep It, or How to Keep Him Wanting More, More, More

> If you are waiting for anything in order to
> live and love without holding back, you suffer.
> Every moment is the most important moment
> of your life.
>
> —*David Deida, author*

One of the biggest secrets to magnetizing men is to have, and keep, a full life. Not as a manipulation, but out of a genuine sense of self-worth and soul purpose. Here's what often happens when you start dating someone you really like. You are excited and feel the urge to see him all the time. Little by little, you find that you're not spending as much time with your own friends or family or even at work. Going to the gym or participating in pastimes you would ordinarily enjoy play second fiddle to seeing your new man. In fact, your time together starts to revolve more and more around his interests than yours. For example, if he's a big sports fan, you'll find yourself spending increasingly more time in sports bars or at his friends' homes watching the games.

After a few short weeks, the relationship becomes the central focus of your life. At first it feels like a dream. But before long, you begin to notice some not-so-dreamy changes. Your friends have stopped calling (because you're never available), you've gained a little weight, and you don't feel as energetic or attractive. Work isn't as exciting as it used to be. Within a couple of months, you feel deadened and resentful, though you're not sure why. Sex isn't as great as it used to be. He's starting to act distant. Right before your eyes, this wonderful new relationship has somehow devolved into what is beginning to look like every other relationship you've had before.

Sound familiar? Many of us have found ourselves, within a few weeks or months of beginning a new relationship, feeling lost and confused, thinking, "What the heck just happened?" You lost yourself, woman, that's what happened. Instead of staying in your life and including your new relationship, you've made the fatal mistake of doing the pretzel dance and twisting yourself into who you think he wants you to be in order to hold on to the relationship and keep him happy.

The pretzel dance approach never works. Altering your behavior or being someone different from who you are is a recipe for disaster. He is attracted to you—the real you— just the way you are, not to some woman who has no life except for him. Here are some more examples of doing the pretzel dance and not keeping your life:

- Breaking plans with your girlfriends to be with him (especially if you lie to yourself or your girlfriends about it)
- Getting to work late and/or leaving early
- No longer working out because it's easier to stay in bed and cuddle
- Quitting activities (classes, organizations, workshops) for which you have a passion
- Dropping off the radar with family and friends
- Failing to make time for anything else but him
- Letting yourself go to pot

Remember, you are a unique individual. You have a purpose on this earth. Twisting yourself up like a pretzel to fit some idea of what you think he wants is not it. Trust me, I know how exciting and intoxicating it is when you meet someone you really like. You want to spend every waking moment with him. While I'm not suggesting you suppress yourself, restrain your passion, or arbitrarily say no to spending time together, I am suggesting that you consider another possibility.

Try including your new romance into your already existing life. Expand your world. Don't shrink to fit his. Trust that when you spend time on your own without him, everything will be fine. (And if it's not, it's probably not the kind of relationship you want anyway.) Time apart between two mature and complete adults only fuels deeper conversations and hotter sexual passion.

The bottom line is that you can have a full life including a successful career, close friends and family, *and* a great relationship. In fact, that is the only way a good relationship will blossom into a magical one. But please understand that getting a life and keeping it is not the same as playing hard to get.

Why "Playing Hard to Get" Doesn't Work

Many dating books over the years have encouraged the tactic of playing hard to get to manipulate men into being interested and attracted. This is dishonest (read: *big* turn-off) and reinforces the false idea that a relationship will somehow save or complete you. If you play hard to get, it may work for a while, but it will never produce the type of long-term, authentic, and satisfying love you really want. Sooner or later, things will start to shift. You'll begin to pressure him, in one way or another, to spend more time with you. When he declines, you'll feel lonely and hurt and wonder what's wrong with the relationship.

Then you'll begin feeling jealous and insecure. You'll become analytical and spend much of your time scheming up ways to get him to prove how much he cares. He'll feel confused and turned off. Rightfully so, he'll wonder what happened to his "hard-to-get" gal who used to have a life. That's about the time he'll pull away, act distant, and give less and less of himself until it blows up into a big fight and you'll wonder why he's changed.

Having Your Own Life and Keeping It = Authentic Irresistibility

This is a new idea you might want to write down. Having your own life is authentically irresistible because it keeps you (and him) from losing yourselves in the relationship. If you imagine that people are like rechargeable batteries, having your own life keeps you fully charged. When you focus all your time and attention only on him, there's no possibility for you to get naturally recharged by life—by other friends, activities, adventures, nature, the universe. Your energy depletes; this is apparent in how you look and feel. You start pulling on him for all of your energy, and he feels exhausted and resentful. The conversations get dull. You begin to nitpick and nag. "What do you want to do?"

and "I don't care—whatever you want to do" is all you ever seem to say to each other.

When you devote all of your time, energy, and attention only to each other, it drains both of you and slowly erodes what could be an otherwise wonderful relationship. Having your own life is a natural way to keep yourself centered so you have more to contribute to your partner and the other important people in and aspects of your life.

Let's be honest. Success is sexy. When you live an inspired and energized life, men naturally find you irresistible because you *are* irresistible. Invest in your health, create community, make a difference, learn new skills, have fun, and share yourself with others. This is what will keep him wanting more, more, more.

Men are no different from women in this respect. They want to be with someone who is expressive, engaged, and active in life. They want a woman who can introduce them to new things and is both interested and interesting.

Get a Life 101: Be an S&M Queen

One way to get a life and keep it is to put energy into being an S&M (success and money) queen. I first heard this term in Karen Salmansohn's fabulous book *The 30-Day Plan to Whip Your Career into Submission*. Here's how to do it: be a star at work. I don't care if you flip burgers at McDonald's or run a Fortune 500 company. Do everything with totality and excellence. Show up on time, all the time. Do what you say you will do. Contribute ideas. Take care of the people around you. Solve problems. Be an agent for change. Invest in being the best in your industry or the best in the world!

If you've been thinking about changing professions, that's even more reason to be a star at your current job. Operating with excellence now will get you back up to speed mentally and energetically so you can hit the ground running in your new position. It will also create good karma. When and if you finally do leave, your current employers will be happy to support you with a great reference and often leave an open door for additional work in the future.

If you're an entrepreneur, look at ways to enhance your business. Is there a new product or service you've wanted to offer? How can you create raving fans by making your customer service sparkle? How can you reach more people with your product or service? Can you impact thousands or even millions more?

Let's not forget the *M* in S&M. Getting a life and keeping it includes having strong financial health as well. This area is crucial because many women delay taking charge of their financial lives as they believe (or have been culturally conditioned to believe) that a man will come along and take care of it for them. This is a setup for disaster. You are an intelligent and capable woman. If you want to fully unleash your irresistibility, invest in your financial health now and don't stop once you get involved in a relationship.

If money management is a challenge for you, I highly recommend my favorite financial coach: David Bach. He is the bestselling author of many books, including *The Automatic Millionaire*, *Smart Women Finish Rich*, and *Smart Couples Finish Rich*. His advice is clear-cut and straightforward, and, most important, it works.

Remember, every relationship is an opportunity to either discover more of your individuality and expand as a human being or do the pretzel dance and twist yourself into a smaller version of you based on who you think your partner wants you to be. Despite what your mind tells you, your partner is attracted to the real you—the authentic you that he first met—not the twisted version you think he wants.

When you commit to being yourself from the start and to communicating your truth no matter what, you'll avoid virtually all the drama, angst, and anxiety of not knowing where things stand that many other women experience on a daily basis. Most women are afraid to be real because they mistakenly believe that they're not enough exactly as they are. This "I'm not enough" mind-set not only is inaccurate but also destroys your well-being and ability to have a loving and satisfying relationship.

Being yourself and speaking your truth from the moment you meet is the secret to having relationships unfold naturally and authentically. It is also the key to maintaining your irresistibility.

Be yourself. Communicate what works for you and what doesn't. Do it from day one and never stop. This is the most powerful step you can take at the beginning of any relationship to set it up for long-term success.

Speaking of relationship success, don't confuse relationship longevity with relationship success. Just because a relationship lasts for many years does not mean it's a success. Many couples cling to a lifeless and miserable existence they call a relationship because they are too afraid to be alone or to face the uncertainty of the unknown. Living a life of quiet desperation devoid of true love, passion, and spiritual partnership is not my idea of success.

Relationships, again, are life's grandest opportunity for spiritual growth and evolution. They exist so that we may discover ourselves, awaken our hearts, and heal our barriers to love. Every relationship you've ever had, or you ever will have, is designed to bring you closer to your divinity and ability to experience and express the very best of who you are.

Irresistible Action Challenge

Use this chapter to expand your possibilities of what it means to live a full life. Recognize that it is possible to have it all. Allow yourself to get used to the idea of including things in your life rather than excluding things. Think "both" rather than "either/or."

1. Take a class or workshop that you've been meaning to take but never got around to. Stop waiting for "someday" and start having a full life now.

2. Investigate how you operate around work and money. Have you been holding back investing in your career or financial health? What steps do you need to take to become an S&M queen?

3. Practice keeping your word with yourself and others, whether or not you are dating right now. When you say that you are going to the gym, go. When you say that you'll show up at a party, show up. This will strengthen your personal power so that when you do have a relationship, you'll be well practiced at keeping your word.

Chapter 11

SECRET 8

Perfect Packaging, or How to Be a Delicious, Scrumptious, Knock-His-Socks-Off, Take-Me-Home-Now Gorgeous Gal 24-7

> The real sin against life is to abuse and destroy beauty, even one's own—even more one's own, for that has been put in our care and we are responsible for its well-being.
>
> —*Katherine Anne Porter,*
> *Pulitzer Prize–winning author*

*L*et's be honest, shall we? No matter how foxy we are on the inside, it's difficult for those of us who are fashionably challenged to really get out there and feel fabulous in the dating game. And while who you are "being" is definitely more important than how you look when it comes to irresistibility (remember poor Sheila?), why sabotage your irresistibility when you don't have to?

Perfect packaging is the art of making your outer appearance a natural and irresistible extension of your inner fox. For those of you who think you've got this department handled, I invite you get over yourself and read on.

What Are You Selling?

Like it or not, we sell ourselves 24-7. Our appearance sells information like our marital status, profession, financial worth, degree of self-worth, age, religion, ethnicity, and intelligence, just to name a few. The clothes you wear, the way you style your hair, and how you put yourself together from head to toe communicate more about you than your words can ever say.

Most of us are blind to what we are selling simply because we're so used to being ourselves. We are unaware of how others perceive us, and friends, family, and associates often don't feel it's their place to give feedback—although that feedback could transform our lives. In a way, it's like watching an episode of Donald Trump's reality show, "The Apprentice." The contestants often have no idea how difficult, unmanageable, cranky, childish, and rude they come across. They are simply being themselves. But to everyone who is watching, it's crystal clear.

Similarly, many women get stuck in a clothing trend or hairstyle and forget to move on with the times. Others are in perpetual pajama-like clothes. Some showcase a flabby tummy when in reality they should cover it up and show off their shapely arms instead. And then there's a certain population who are simply clueless when it comes to fashion and unfortunately no one is around to say, "You're fired!"

Thank goodness you don't need a reality TV show to discover the art of perfect packaging. All it takes is an open mind, a desire to explore, and a willingness to try on new possibilities. A style-savvy friend or professional image consultant can quickly and painlessly help you see yourself in a new light. As my client Heather discovered, you're either selling "Come 'n' get me, baby" or "I'm *so* not interested."

Heather's Story

One day I was sitting across from my client Heather, a forty-something environmental consultant who said she was ready for a relationship. Her career was cruising along, she owned her apartment in NYC, and she had a blossoming social life. She asked me, "What am I doing wrong, Marie? Guys just don't seem interested in me."

"I'm not surprised," I said. "You're not exactly selling 'I'm a hot available babe looking for a relationship.' It's more like you're selling 'I'm a dumpy middle-aged woman with zero interest in men.'" No one was able to see her inner babe-ness behind the fashion catastrophe she had created to hide it. Heather, an attractive, successful, and loving woman, was hiding her voluptuous, full-figured body underneath ill-fitting, high-waisted jeans and baggy, faded men's T-shirts. She wore dusty brown clogs and a yellow kerchief around her head. Not exactly a come-hither look. Heather was interested in getting honest feedback and did not hurt herself with my remarks. She took a look for herself and discovered that, ironically, she was purposefully dressing frumpy to keep men away. While she believed she wanted a relationship, in reality she was terrified of the potential rejection inherent in the dating game. In that moment, however, Heather realized that her desire for love and intimacy outweighed her fear of rejection. By not judging herself for what she discovered, she instantly became excited about a new, more stylish look. Since that conversation, Heather has begun to wear colorful, feminine tops and flowing skirts that complement her voluptuous figure. Instead of clogs, she now wears beautiful sandals and other comfortable, well-made shoes. Her clothing and accessory choices are now more appropriate for the beautiful and available woman she is. She no longer wears kerchiefs and instead allows her beautiful curly brown hair to be seen.

She is taking regular salsa classes and goes shopping with fashion-conscious friends who support her in finding great clothes for her budget and body type.

The bottom line is this. How you look impacts how you feel. You can package yourself to either support your inner irresistibility or suppress it. And supporting your irresistibility does not mean dressing provocatively or inappropriately for your age or taste. It's about taking care of yourself in a way that's in concert with your desire to be irresistible and have satisfying relationships with men. It's about bringing awareness to how you communicate to the world who you are through your appearance.

Perfect packaging comes down to awareness. Here are a few questions to consider to get your juices flowing:

- Do you wear clothes that actually make you look and feel attractive or do you pray that someone will notice your inner goddess underneath the layers of T-shirts, baggy sweaters, and sweatpants?
- When was the last time you went through your closet and got rid of old, unattractive, and unflattering items?
- Do you wear makeup? When was the last time you updated your cosmetics?
- How about your figure? Do you maintain a strong and fit body or do you hide your babe-ness behind a layer of unhealthy extra weight?

■ Do you know how to dress for your body type? How clear are you on what you should not be wearing?

Perfect Packaging Resources

Looking good is all about making the most of what you've got. Learn to use your assets to your advantage. One option is to hire a personal image consultant. For a set fee, she or he will help you go through your wardrobe and edit it down to keep only what works best for you. Most will also shop with you for new clothes and help you put together appropriate looks to take you from desk to date.

A less expensive route is to consult books. I particularly love the *What Not to Wear* gals, Trinny Woodall and Susannah Constantine. They appear regularly on "Oprah" and have written several books designed to help women use clothing to look and feel their best. Trinny and Susannah are excellent guides who will help you get real on what's working and what's not when it comes to your wardrobe; they can show you, step-by-step, that changing the way you dress can truly change your life.

Magazines can also be an excellent source of inspiration and guidance for the fashion challenged. Look for magazines that provide websites, phone numbers, store locations, and prices for the items they feature. Many magazines also offer the same look at different price points to serve every budget. Finally, never underestimate the power of a fashion intervention. Invite a few good friends over to help you update your wardrobe and discover what works best for you now.

Hair and Makeup

Along the same lines as clothing, your hair and makeup play a big part in how confident and attractive you feel. With the overwhelming array of cosmetic products available on the market, it's easy to get confused and resist buying anything new. A simple way to discover what makeup works best for you now is to visit a beauty counter at a high-end department store. Here's what to do: choose a brand that you feel best suits your individual style and that falls within your budget. Schedule a makeup lesson and be clear about what you are there for. If you only plan to purchase one or two items, let the makeup artist know in advance. She or he will appreciate your honesty. Be sure to take note of how to apply the products so you can easily re-create the look again by yourself. If high-end anything is outside of your financial plan, you can get similar results from drug store cosmetics. Use magazines for inspiration, product recommendations, color suggestions, and how-tos.

I like to keep things very simple. A touch of gloss, a sweep of mascara, and a hint of color on your eyes and cheeks can take you from drab to fab in minutes. When it comes to makeup, less is definitely more. A little makeup applied tastefully and skillfully goes a long way. Women are naturally beautiful, especially when they are practiced at living an irresistible lifestyle.

Regarding your hair, go for the best. A fantastic haircut will showcase your best facial features and save you time and energy getting ready every day. Get a trim at least every six weeks—more often if you have color or highlights done. I like to use the products my stylist recommends. This does away with the guesswork, and for the few extra bucks, a consistently polished look is worth it.

Remember, Everything Matters

Irresistible women pay attention to the details. Become practiced at treating yourself like a beautiful diamond that sparkles with a little polishing. Commit to having everything you own be in great shape—especially you.

In life, everything matters. It's no different with your appearance. Healthy skin is just as important as healthy hair. Great shoes are just as important as great clothes. Nice bras are as important as nice socks. Investigate your wardrobe, your cosmetic bag, and your jewelry box. Look for rips, stains, or wear and tear that's beyond repair. Get rid of anything that doesn't make you look and feel your best. Take inventory of your shoes, bags, bras, and underwear. Keep an eye open for items that are worn out or that no longer work for you. If you feel embarrassed wearing something or would feel self-conscious if someone saw you in it, don't hesitate to chuck it.

Simply become aware of details and commit to keeping your appearance clean and crisp. I'm not suggesting you adopt an obsessive-compulsive striving for perfection, but experience the sense of personal ease and satisfaction that comes with having things around you be well taken care of.

Don't forget to give yourself a gentle once-over. Go to the mirror and look at your skin, eyebrows, and teeth. If you could use some professional support in any of these areas, get it. Go for a facial, have your eyebrows shaped, and pay a visit to the dentist. As a self-proclaimed makeover show addict, I've seen more before and after shots than you can imagine. One of the fastest and easiest ways to brighten your appearance is by having your teeth whitened. Whether it's a professional job or do-it-yourself whitening strips from the drugstore, I never cease to be amazed at what a difference a fresh, white smile makes.

Most important, don't rush as you get ready for your day. Apply your makeup carefully. Allow enough time to wash and style your hair so you look and feel fresh. Choose clothing and accessories that make you feel fantastic.

Do what you know will support your irresistibility inside and out. Drink water, take vitamins, and wear sunscreen. Nourish yourself with healthy, nutrient-rich food that fuels you.

With so many books, videos, and magazines available regarding health and fitness, I'm not about to go into great detail about what to do; however, suffice to say, your body is designed to move. Never underestimate the impact that consistent exercise has on your irresistibility. The benefits of fitness go way beyond having a strong and healthy figure. From increased endorphins (a.k.a. happy hormones) that naturally combat depression, to reduced risk of heart disease, to increased ability to perform everyday functions, the payoff is well worth the investment.

Irresistible Action Challenge

Make a list of different areas of your packaging that need updating. The following will give you some ideas:

- bras and underwear
- cosmetics and skin care and hair products
- jewelry and accessories
- shoes
- work clothes
- evening clothes
- workout clothes
- hair, skin, and teeth
- socks
- jackets and coats

Now select one area. Get out everything that is related to that category. Try things on and see what works for you now.

Strength training, cardiovascular exercise, and flexibility conditioning are the three keys to fitness. Choose forms of exercise that incorporate all of these elements. Find classes and activities you find motivating and fun. As a dancer, I prefer classes that rock it out with heart-pumping music. I also love the intense challenge and spiritual nature of yoga. Of course, the most important thing in any exer-

Donate, give away, or throw away things you haven't worn or used within the past ten months. Don't forget to make note of things you'd like to replace.

Look in catalogs and magazines, online, and in stores for more current and appropriate choices that will support your irresistibility. Don't rush this process. Take your time and replace pieces as you find them. Use your intuition and fashion-savvy friends to guide you in choosing what works best. This is an excellent activity to do with others. If you want to capture a visual of your irresistible transformation, take before and after pictures.

Once you've completed one area, choose another and repeat the process. Keep going until everything you own is a clear and current expression of your most irresistible self. Have fun with this challenge! Before you know it, you'll have completely updated your look from head to toe.

cise program is to show up with consistency. If you haven't exercised in a while, I know how intimidating it can be to get started. Trust me. Nothing will make a bigger difference in the way you look and feel. One of the best ways to set yourself up for success is by going to classes. The energy and efficiency of groups are unbeatable. Classes are usually about an hour long, and you get an incredible total body workout while being coached and motivated by a professional instructor and others on the same path with you. Remember that you are a tri-part being—a mind, body, and soul. Why sell yourself short? Everything you do is either supporting your irresistibility or suppressing it. Go for the triple threat, baby. Use all of your assets to fully express your aliveness and irresistibility.

ⅢⅢⅢⅢ Irresistible Insight Questions ⅢⅢⅢⅢ

1. What areas of your personal packaging could use some attention?

2. What kind of support do you need?

3. When was the last time you updated your wardrobe? Cosmetics? Hair?

4. Is there anything you own that embarrasses you?

5. Are you willing to let those items go to make room for something newer and more irresistible?

Part 3

Pulling It All Together

If we are facing in the right direction,
all we have to do is keep on walking.

—Ancient Buddhist proverb

Chapter 12

FAQs: Twenty-One Answers to Your Most Burning Dating Dilemmas

Do you ever wonder if your questions are silly? I've certainly wondered about mine. Especially around hot-button subjects like intimacy, sex, and love. I've often asked myself, "Am I the only one who doesn't know the answer to this?"

Over the years, I've been privileged to receive many questions from women around the world. I always admire the courage it takes to reach out and ask for support. That desire to gain a deeper understanding of oneself and the people around you is what lays the foundation for a lifetime of growth.

Following are a composite of the most common questions I've received. They provide general guidance based on the Make Every Man Want You approach.

1. Why can't I let go of my ex?

Because you're resisting the breakup. Remember, anything you resist persists. Whatever you truly see, without judging, disappears. Either you can continue to torture yourself and everyone around you by resisting reality or you can see that it's over (and not judge yourself for that fact), which allows those feelings to naturally dissolve. In the meantime, start having some fun and behave like the irresistible fox you know you are.

2. Why am I so distrusting of men?

Because somewhere you learned to distrust men. There are three ways in which we absorb information as we grow up: we hear it, see it, or experience it. If you were raised in a family in which you repeatedly heard that men can't be trusted, you will most likely have this hardwired into your belief system. If during your childhood you saw that men can't be trusted by witnessing your father or other male figures lie or cheat, you will most likely be predisposed to mistrust men. Finally, if as a child you experienced that men can't be trusted—either by some form of abuse or by male role models breaking their word—you are, once again, likely predisposed to mistrust men. All of this is quite normal, and, thank goodness, the only thing you need to dissolve this belief is awareness.

3. Why am I obsessed with him cheating on me?

This is a tricky one. Partially because of preconditioned beliefs, as just discussed. But there's another piece to this. I've found it helps to pay close attention to the specific situation and relationship. One possibility is that you're intuitively picking up on the fact that he cannot be trusted and may indeed be cheating. You've got to be willing to investigate your internal information and see if it's coming from your thoughts (like habitual insecurity that is unrelated to current events) or that funny feeling inside when you just know something is not right (called a gut instinct or intuition). It all comes down to being willing to investigate your own personal landscape and, most important, to tell yourself the truth—even if it's not convenient or what you want to believe.

4. Does an age difference matter?

Not unless you make it matter. Nothing has meaning except for the meaning you give it. Stereotyping men by age is as ridiculous as stereotyping men by hair color or shoe size. If you want to be truly irresistible, drop all your baggage about age and start getting interested in people for who they really are.

5. Do guys like it when a woman makes the first move?

Depends. If you come on like gangbusters because deep down you believe a relationship will solve all your problems, then the answer is no. If you are centered, alive, and irresistible, then the answer is yes.

If you happen to lay it on a man who has a "story" that he needs to be the aggressor, then it may be a problem (and who wants him anyway?). Most mature, well-adjusted, single men appreciate unsolicited feminine attention.

6. Do guys secretly want us to change them?

No.

7. Do men like it when women ask them out?

Some men do and some don't. As you've learned from the rest of the book, rules don't work. The key to being truly irresistible is to forget about following rules and develop your ability to look and see what's appropriate right now. Use your most powerful tool—your intuition—to guide you on a case-by-case basis.

8. Do men like it when women say what they want in bed?

Yes, yes, and, oh yeah . . . yes. Two caveats: (1) do *not* refer to what your former partners used to do and (2) do *not* speak to him in a condescending way as though he should already know what it is that you want.

9. Do men really prefer dating skinny women?

Nope. Men prefer hot and desirous women of every shape and size. Some men like a little extra cushion for the pushin', some like them lean and mean, and some like everything in between. No matter what your size, be irresistibly you by taking great care of yourself inside and out.

10. Does it work to play hard to get?

No. Reread Chapter 10.

11. How can I get my man to be more affectionate?

You can't. Men are "as-is" merchandise. Love 'em or leave 'em, baby (reread Chapter 2). Don't waste your time or energy trying to change or improve anyone.

12. How do I know when a man's not interested?

If he never to rarely calls or he wants you to always call him; if he never asks to see you or insists you come to see him; if he says he's too busy, he just got out of another relationship and needs time, he's got "intimacy issues," or he doesn't want to have sex with you, then you can pretty much bet he's not interested.

13. How soon is too soon to bring a new guy home to meet my parents?

There's no hard and fast timing rule for appropriateness to meet the parents. However, most women rush this meeting because they have high hopes for the future and are trying to force a relationship to get to the next level. The best thing for you, him, and your family is for you to relax. Trying to push things along because you think you'll be happier and more connected once they meet is a recipe for disaster. If he's really "the one," meeting your folks will happen very naturally all on its own.

14. If a woman calls a guy after the first date, will he be turned off?

Guys are turned off by desperation and neediness. So, if you are being desperate and needy when you call, yes, he will be turned off. If you have the idea that a relationship will save you, yes, he will be turned off. If you have to call right away because you are a control freak and consider yourself a strong and independent woman who has no time for games and you need to know immediately if he likes you or not, yes, he will be turned off. But if you are free from manipulation and expectations, then, no, he probably will not be turned off. The trick is not to lie to yourself. Also, don't forget that men are natural hunters that love a little chase. Don't rob him of the pleasure he gets from acting out his primal, male instincts.

15. Is it OK to ask my boyfriend about his ex-girlfriends?

Yes, if you want to torture yourself. Asking about his ex only sends his mind back to thinking of her. When, and if, the time is appropriate to talk about exes (his or yours), communicate from a place of neutrality and awareness. Practice true listening and do not bad-mouth your ex or his. Until then, why dig up something that's over? Keep your attention in the moment and discover who he is in relationship to you.

16. Is there anything guys don't like doing in bed?

With the possible exception of bringing in other men (and some heterosexual guys are into that), most men like it all. Your job is to make sure that you are clean and fresh but, most important, that you initiate playful sexual exploration and mutual discovery of what works best for you as a couple.

17. What does a guy really think when you have sex on the first date?

It all depends. If you are having sex as a manipulation to create deep feelings, to get him to like you and/or love you, or you give it up because you're drunk, he's not going to be thinking, "Gee, can't wait to take this one home to Mom!" Men are not stupid. They know if you are using sex as a device and will either play along to get more sex or conveniently forget to call you for a month or two until they want it again. Either way, he will write you off as nonrelationship material and you'll be forever slotted in his f*^k buddy category.

When you are clear and centered and are not thinking that a relationship will save you, sex on the first date can be exhilarating and fun. Most women, however, still believe on some level that a relationship will save them. My suggestion is, when in doubt, wait it out.

18. What does it mean when a guy says that he loves you but he's not in love with you?

It means he wants out and doesn't have the courage to say it straight. He's trying his best to let you down easy and not hurt your feelings any more than he has to.

19. What does it mean when he says that he's not ready for a serious relationship?

It means he doesn't want a serious relationship with you. Don't kid yourself on this one or hang around and have sex with him until he's ready. Run, don't walk, outta there and get your irresistible a$$ back on the market.

20. What does he mean when he says that he needs space?

It means he wants to date other women or at least get far enough away from you that he has that option. Don't make the mistake of believing he's different because of all of his special career, familial, and health complexities (blah, blah, blah). A man who truly wants you and knows how fabulous you are can't bear the thought of not seeing you for weeks or months. There are plenty of single men out there who are dying for a hot, irresistible babe like you to keep as close as possible.

21. How can I be sure I'm with the right guy?

You can't. Unless you fully invest in the relationship you've got right now, you'll never know. There's an adage that says, "The grass is always greener where you water it." Until you start giving your current relationship the attention it deserves, you'll remain in a painful space of second-guessing, thinking about what you should or shouldn't do. Stop holding back and start being completely honest, compassionate, and loving toward the person you're with. The relationship will either move ahead or it won't. You can't figure this out in your mind—you need to fully engage with your heart. Only then will you discover your truth.

Chapter 13

Now What?

ongratulations, Miss Irresistible! You have now discovered the secrets to making every man want you and have the tools to enjoy healthy and satisfying relationships with men.

In Part 1, you passed Irresistibility 101 and discovered not only why you need to be irresistible but also what a powerful impact you are meant to have in the world. You also discovered that relationships are spiritual opportunities, and while they can be glorious, having a relationship will not save or complete you. You also learned that now is all you've got, men are "as-is" merchandise, and, despite what our minds fight for, love cannot be guaranteed.

In Part 2, you discovered how to ditch the rules and trash your perfect man checklist. You learned how to disengage from the treacherous gender war and how to let go of stories from the past that you are somehow defective or damaged. You discovered that dropping your complaints will help you meet more men instantly and why getting a life and keeping it are key to staying centered and irresistible in any relationship. Finally, you explored the idea of perfect packaging and discovered easy ways to make your outer appearance an irresistible extension of your inner goddess. Remember, you can be spiritually, emotionally, and sexually self-expressive right now. In fact, this is the real secret to authentic and lasting irresistibility. You must recognize that you are whole and complete in this moment. Live as though this is it. While it's exciting to unleash your aliveness, it's also a tremendous gift to the world. By letting your own irresistibility shine, you give others permission to do the same.

Now that you have this wisdom, don't keep it a secret. Tell every woman you know that there's another possibility. Tell them they don't have to manipulate or play games to get what they want with men. Tell them they don't have to be fake or strategic to experience all the love, attention, and satisfaction they desire. When you come across a woman who is lost and searching for a better way, speak up and share the insight from *Make Every Man Want You*.

You may be wondering what happened with that fantastic man Josh I told you about. Remember, the guy who pretty much scored a zero on my perfect man checklist? Well, not so long ago we were having dinner at our beach house in Sag Harbor, New York. It was late summer; the orange light of sunset danced on our wine glasses while the trees softly rustled in the warm breeze. It was a typical evening for us; we sat cross-legged on our couch, eating a home-cooked meal and watching a movie. This night, however, turned out to be very special. Just a few minutes into the movie, Josh quietly set aside his plate, put down his wine glass, and got down on one knee. He smiled, took my hand, and asked me to marry him.

In that instant, I knew he wasn't asking a woman who had "followed the rules" and manipulated him into a proposal. I knew he wasn't asking a woman who had skillfully pressured him into marriage. I knew he wasn't asking a figment of his imagination or some manufactured perfect-wife persona. He was asking me—the real, flawed, sometimes crazy, and often irresistible me. The woman who laughs, cries, makes mistakes, loves cheese, is obsessed with tweezing stray hairs, and cooks one heck of a crab cake.

When I could finally speak, I squeezed his hand, looked him directly in the eye, and said, "Yes, I'll marry you!" It was one of the sweetest and most lovely moments in my life.

Does this mean we'll blissfully ride off into happily-ever-after land? Who knows. My only job is to stay here and tell the truth, in this moment, and the future will take care of itself. What I do know is this: being as honest, compassionate, and loving as I can be is the secret to my true irresistibility. My life works when my heart is open. It keeps me sane and on track. When I'm vulnerable, I'm beautiful.

When I'm expressive and real about who I am right now, I feel alive down to the very core of my being. I'm connected, both to myself and to the people around me.

Whatever you do, don't hold back your heart. Your capacity to love is greater than you could ever imagine. Your irresistibility is a gift. And your willingness to love and be irresistible is a miracle that touches us all.

Additional Resources

*D*on't forget to download your complimentary Irresistible Action Guide that includes all the exercises in this book as well as a four-week audio coaching program to keep you inspired and on track with the Make Every Man Want You approach. Visit makeeveryman wantyou.com/actionguide now to access these free bonus resources and more.

To learn about Marie's other products and programs, visit marieforleo.com.

Bach, David. *The Automatic Millionaire: A Powerful One-Step Plan to Live and Finish Rich.* New York: Broadway, 2003.

Bach, David. *Smart Women Finish Rich: 9 Steps to Achieving Financial Security and Funding Your Dreams.* New York: Broadway, 2003.

Chopra, Deepak. *The Seven Spiritual Laws of Success: A Practical Guide to the Fulfillment of Your Dreams.* Novato, CA: New World Library, 1995.

Kane, Ariel, and Shya Kane. *Working on Yourself Doesn't Work: A Book About Instantaneous Transformation.* New York: McGraw-Hill, 2009.

Katie, Byron, and Stephen Mitchell. *Loving What Is: Four Questions That Can Change Your Life.* New York: Three Rivers Press, 2003.

Tolle, Eckhart. *The Power of Now: A Guide to Spiritual Enlightenment.* Novato, CA: New World Library, 1999.

Woodall, Trinny, Susannah Constantine, and Robin Matthews. *What Not to Wear.* New York: Riverhead Books, 2003.

Index

About the Author

*M*arie Forleo is a dynamic entrepreneur who teaches people how to be fully authentic, expressive, and alive through the power of being present. A savvy speaker with a tell-it-like-it-is approach, Marie has a style that appeals to a wide, diverse audience. Breaking traditional molds, Marie launched a multifaceted career as an author, speaker, lifestyle coach, dancer/choreographer, and fitness professional.

Her work has appeared in the *New York Times*, *Shape Magazine*, and *Healthy & Fit* and on CNN.com, Forbes.com, and HSN. She has done countless interviews on radio and TV. As a dancer/choreographer and fitness professional, she works with legendary companies such as MTV, VH1, and Nike and partners with leading women's magazines such as *Self*, *Women's Health*, and *Prevention Magazine*. She has four top-selling fitness videos and is proud to be a Nike Elite Dance Athlete and Master Trainer.

Marie's clients include millionaire entrepreneurs, corporate executives, creative professionals, and stay-at-home moms who want excellence and well-being in mind, body, and soul.

A born-and-raised Jersey girl, Marie now happily splits her time living in New York City's West Village and "out east" in the Hamptons with her favorite actor, Josh, and her favorite new young actor, Zane.

Learn more about Marie at marieforleo.com.